S0-CAP-824

Bridges:

The People Changing America

A COMPILATION OF INSPIRING AUTHORS

Edited by Rev. Dr. Jim Milley

Bridges: The People Changing America

Copyright ©2018 Bridges Publishing

All rights reserved.

Disclaimer No part of this publication may be copied, reproduced in any format, by any means, electronic or otherwise, without prior consent from the copyright owner and publisher of this book.

www.BridgesUS.org

For Information:

Bridges dba for Network of Community Entrepreneurs
466 Foothill Blvd #320
La Canada Flintridge, CA 91011

In conjunction with
GWYW Publishing
1230 Crescent Dr.
Glendale, CA 91205

Table of Contents

It is my sincere hope that the stories in this book will help you experience the life transformation which you are seeking.

Dedication

This book is dedicated to all the people serving as Bridges who bring us together, with one another and with God, while simultaneously embracing our differences.

Partnership Appreciation

Bridges gives thanks for the partnership of Geneva Presbyterian Church in the production and distribution of this book. Your encouragement, prayers, friendship, and support have sustained us in lean times and multiplied our impact in times of feasting. Through our ever-expanding partnership, may God bring together many diverse peoples who experience relationships filled with authentic disclosure, grace, forgiveness, love, joy, and hope, all for the glory of the Triune God and the benefit of the many peoples across America.

About the Cover

Bridges are not structures but people-people who have been changed on the inside through the joyful and difficult work of building relationships in a second or third culture. These people carry within them an ability to identify compassionately with others. These Bridge Leaders have the ability to move back and forth between groups and so can stand with multiple language groups, religious groups, political parties, and even countries. Because of who they have become, Bridges can bring us together.

Bridges are shaped and inspired by the prayer that Jesus prayed to God the Father:

> *As you sent me into the world, so I have sent them into the world...I in them and you in me, that they may become perfectly one, so that the world may know that you sent me and loved them even as you loved me. (John 17:21-23)*

People become Bridges, and Bridges can bring us together.

How To Read This Book

I invite you to approach the reading of this book with anticipation, expectation, and hope.

The stories, Scriptures, questions, and prayers in this book are waiting for you. There is a place and time that the Spirit of God is planning to meet you. If the Spirit of God does meet you, your life will be changed.

There are multiple ways to read this book. None of them are necessarily wrong—nor necessarily right. Much depends on how we read and our inner state of being when we read.

And yet there are ways to read these stories that, through centuries of repeated use, have proven to be more likely to create the space and time where God moves within us and changes us—forever.

Here is one such way to read this book. The Bridges Community often follows this series of steps in groups of four to six people, but these steps can also be used by an individual. Create safe and sacred space for yourself by following these ten steps

1. Create a safe and sacred space for yourself
2. Pray for God's help
3. Read the story
4. Reflect with some questions
5. Read the Scripture(s)
6. Reflect with some questions
7. Decide what you want to do next and write it down
8. Go forth and take action
9. Sometime later, talk to someone about the experience of trying to take action

10. Reflect on, perhaps even write down in a journal, what you learned from your action or resistance to action. Afterwards, repeat the above ten-step cycle

It may be clear to you how to take some of these ten steps, while others may be shrouded in unfamiliar language.

Allow me to explain a few of the above steps in a little more detail.

"Safe and sacred space" usually needs some explanation. I recently enjoyed sitting under Santa Monica pier with my feet in the sand and the waves lapping at the pilings. It was safe because I had no fear of being harassed or threatened by anyone. It was sacred because I had the sense that God could show up to me at any time, in a thought, a person, a word, or a still small voice. If you can find or create a safe and sacred space, use it with joy.

If you cannot find a safe and sacred space externally, seek to create that space in your heart, mind, soul, and body. For example, some moms find that driving the minivan is the only meditation time they are going to get. The key is to create a time and space where you can think your own thoughts, feel safe, and believe that God has the ability to show up in your experience.

Praying is simply talking to God, listening to God, and sitting silently with God. Before reading or reflecting, say a short prayer and invite God to speak to you and change you through this experience of reading and reflecting.

The pattern of the ten steps is very important. We call the pattern the Bridges' Learning Cycle. It is easy to follow the pattern after a few practice runs around the cycle. First, read the story. Resist the urge to read the scripture first. Then spend some time reflecting using the questions provided. Next, read the biblical story or passage. Spend some time reflecting again using the provided questions. Resist the urge to read quickly and rush off. The reflection time is key-reflecting on both the story and the scripture.

You will discover that the entire pattern helps you reflect on your own life as well.

Before ending your time, be sure to decide what action you want to take as a result of what you have experienced. Write down that action. Share it with a friend.

This is the Bridges' Learning Cycle—prayer followed by story followed by reflection followed by Scripture followed by reflection followed by prayer followed by ACTION.

And then, ACTION is followed by a repetition of the Bridges' Learning Cycle, beginning with the question, "What happened when I acted?" Or if you didn't act, "What did I learn from my own resistance to acting?"

Using the Bridges' Learning Cycle helps us avoid religious activity that has no impact on ourselves, others, or our communities and nations.

The book of James describes what people are like when they hear the Word of God but go away without reflecting and without a plan of action:

> *23For if you listen to the Word and do not obey, it is like glancing at your face in a mirror. 24 You see yourself, walk away, and forget what you look like. 25 But if you look carefully into the perfect law that sets you free, and if you do what it says and don't forget what you heard, then God will bless you for doing it. (James 1:22-25)*

We would like to be the kind of people that look in the mirror, see that our hair is messed up, and promptly get a brush. It is a great accomplishment for many of us to look in the mirror. And yet, just looking does not necessarily lead to change. That is why we are praying and asking God to empower us by the Holy Spirit to make the changes in our lives that lead to life, joy, and meaningful service to others.

The book of James does not avoid stating the truth plainly: "Don't just listen to God's Word. You must do what it says. Otherwise, you are only fooling yourselves." There are many people who are fooling themselves, but the fact that you have read this far means you are already on the path towards accepting whatever you discover in the mirror and allowing God to change you.

May the Spirit of the Living God meet you as you read, reflect, and take action. May the God who raised Jesus from the dead empower you to respond to what the Spirit is saying to you through the words of this book and through your reflections.

Introduction
The Friends Changing America

By Rev. Dr. Jim Milley

When I was somewhere between eleven and sixteen years old, my mom and dad were, well, not available. Every morning for five years I threw my two newspaper routes and fed myself breakfast. When I stepped out the front door to walk to the school bus stop at 9:00 a.m. my mom was still in bed, struggling with her own mental darkness. My dad was either off to work or simply never came home the night before.

And yet I thrived. I thrived because the ladies from the church would come visit my mom and bring us casseroles. The neighbors across the street let me watch the Flyers beat the Maple Leafs for the 3rd Stanley Cup in a row on their big screen TV. Mr. L from the church helped me with my first term paper in 9th grade. Mr. B, two doors down, let us camp at his house when the heat at our house was turned off. Mrs. C taught me about dating her daughter, the first of more than a few young women I met at the church. Mr. S not only taught me saxophone at school but also invited me to play during worship at the church. And then I lived in his RV next to his home for a summer. Over twenty families in the neighborhood hired me to mow their grass, shovel their snow, and sometimes rake their leaves.

I had a great big community! I had five dads and six moms. I had people watching out for me whose names I didn't even know.

This was the America I knew back then.

Today, we seem afraid. We seem divided. We seem alone. In three years, three desperate teens have jumped off the roofs of local high schools within ten miles of my home. Over ten school shootings occurred across the country this year, which has only just started. Fifty-eight thousand homeless people in Los Angeles County are living in the wind and cold while town hall meetings are being organized to "clean up" the problem.

Something is wrong in America.

But what you have in your hand is a sign of something new. It is a sign of hope. And this hope flows through real people in real neighborhoods making everyday decisions to share that hope. I am very privileged to call some of these people my friends.

Through this book I would like to introduce you to some of my friends. I have come to believe that these friends are changing America. It is still hidden because not everyone feels, sees, knows, or believes it. This book will give you an opportunity to recognize the transformation. These friends are building relationships, shaping lives, forming groups, and improving communities, one relationship at a time. Every one of their stories will help you to feel, see, know, believe, and maybe even begin to find a way to experience it.

These friends, these Bridge Leaders, are not paid employees of a large nonprofit, new government program, or billionaire's new corporate dream. These leaders are not full-time religious leaders, social workers, or counselors—rather, they are people just like you and me: mothers and fathers, teens, retired engineers, semi-employed pastors, mechanics, apartment managers, lawyers, schoolteachers, homemakers, and more. Yet they have found a way to make a tremendous difference, not necessarily through great things but through everyday things.

What these Bridge Leaders do have is a sense of compassionate urgency, not obligation or drudgery. It is a personal commitment driven by energy and zest; a deep passion accompanied by a realization that there is nothing else in the world that they would rather be doing. Indeed, many describe this urgency as a call from

God that compels them to persevere when others would feel at peace with quitting or turning back.

I have the privilege of leading Bridges, which is the nonprofit organization that serves these Bridge Leaders. As of the compiling of this book, Bridges has equipped over 100 leaders and currently supports about seventy-five ministries in four states. Many of us have gathered from all over America to champion these leaders with coaching, training, support groups, counseling, tax-deductible status, organizational development, strategic planning, marketing, donations, accounting, and any ongoing support that they require. We recognize that Bridges is simply the resource organization for our friends who are serving a great diversity of peoples in America today. Each of them requires community and connection with God—the stories that follow will explain a lot more about this.

I pray that my friends and their stories both nurture and disrupt your life. First, I hope their stories inspire you to support Bridges and these Bridge Leaders in any way you can. But even more importantly, I hope they create an urgency in you to ask yourself some of the questions which I myself find consistently both disrupting and nurturing. How can our everyday lives be part of something much bigger than the stereotypical American Dream?

What is God calling us to do in our everyday lives, right where we are, with the people we see? Are we willing to listen carefully to the deeper questions of the people in our homes, on our street, in our building, on our commute, at the club, and next door? Will we make the effort to open ourselves to feel the pain of people in the check-out line, chat room, or cafe?

Are we willing to ask ourselves: "Where is God in the heart of this situation?", "Whom has God called me to love and serve?", and "How can we revive the types of communities in which we thrive?"

Bridge Leaders are creating friendships, and these friendships are creating better neighbors. Being better neighbors brings us together. Coming together gives us a sense of hope, community, security. We don't have to live with division, loneliness, and fear. God didn't intend it that way. I hope you truly enjoy these stories and share them with others.

With hope and joy,

Jim

Rev. Dr. Jim Milley
Chief Catalyst
Bridges dba for Network of Community Entrepreneurs
466 Foothill Blvd #320
La Canada Flintridge, CA 91011
Jim@BridgesUS.org
www.BridgesUS.org
@tweetbridges
#bridgeleaders
#bridgesus

Chapter 1

On the Soccer Field: A Coach, An Ex-Con, and A Judge

By Coach

Prayer of Invitation

Gracious God, thank you for making it possible for me to be with you today. Thank you for never leaving me nor forsaking me.
I invite you to speak to me a word that transforms me.
I invite you to touch within me a spot that needs to be healed.
I invite you to move me to do the things that you want done in our world.
Use this time to get me ready for whatever is coming next.
Amen

Parents were cheering like crazy, and the kids were playing hard, giving it their all on the soccer field. As I coached my son's soccer team, it was hard not to think about how much was at stake. We needed to win this to make the playoffs. But it wasn't looking good. My son's team was behind, and it was beginning to look like we weren't going to win this game. While normally I might start to panic, and maybe even lose my cool in a game like this, today I was calmer and more relaxed than usual. While losing an important game was nothing new for me as a coach, what was new for me today was that I was trying out a new perspective.

I had just finished a Bible study in the book of Mark, where I had been blown away by how much amazing stuff happened with Jesus and his disciples in the course of their everyday lives. Of all the thoughts running through my head after that Bible study, one of the big ideas was that Jesus was at work everywhere in the world, not just inside the walls of the church. After finishing that study, I made a conscious decision to try and see God at work outside the walls of my church. Coaching soccer was one of the first places I looked for God at work, starting with this game.

My son's team didn't win that day. So much for seeing God at work outside the church, I thought. After giving the kids a pep talk under the shade of a tree after the game, I headed off, still hoping God would show up. As I was leaving the field, I crossed paths with the head referee of our match. We stopped and chatted for a few moments and found out we had a similar faith. As we talked, we both quickly concluded that more could be done on a spiritual level to support the kids, families, and volunteers of this soccer league. So, the head referee and I decided to get together for prayer and invite other soccer dads to join us.

One of the dads I invited to that prayer group was my friend Barrett. Barrett is an amazing turnaround story for Christ. He was in and out of prison more times than he can remember, dealing drugs, stealing, and running from the law. One day Barrett got his act together after being beaten almost to death by someone with a baseball bat.

A year before joining the prayer group for soccer dads, there was a significant day in Barrett's life when he had to appear in court to wrap up some probation issues and deal with fines that he owed the county for all the crimes he had committed over the years. I remember that day like it was yesterday. My wife, Barrett's wife, a few close friends, and I were all praying that the courts would deal with Barrett favorably so that he could continue to move forward with his life of recovery and impact. I'll never forget when Barrett called me that day after court. I stepped out of a meeting to take his call, and he told me that he had just left the court and the judge had looked favorably upon him. The judge saw Barrett's progress and spoke to how he was married, back in school, paying child support, working at a church, and doing good things with his life. Instead of enforcing the fines, penalties, and probation, the judge waived all of Barrett's fines, penalties, and restrictions and affirmed him as a member of society once again. We were all blown away.

Barrett was the last one to enter our prayer meeting that morning. We were gathered in my dining room chatting, just about to start, when Barrett walked in the door. Barrett immediately said to the referee, "I know you... We've met before." It turned out that the referee with whom I started the prayer group for soccer dads was, unbeknownst to me, the judge who had looked favorably on Barrett in court a year ago.

So here we were, a group of dads—including an ex-con, a judge, and me, the coach—praying for each other... praying for the soccer league, the families, the kids, the volunteers, and one another. As I listened to the men pray, I thought back to that soccer game, and how I had held so much at stake with the score, and how intensely I had been searching to see God at work outside of my church walls. While we were all quietly praying for one another and the families of this soccer league, I felt like cheering.

1. What was the coach looking for at the soccer game in the beginning of the story? What was Jon hoping for?

2. In what way does the story suggest that God showed up at the soccer field?

3. In what ways have you noticed God in your everyday life? (Think about your time at home, the office, the coffee shop, the sport field, the gym, the yoga studio, the doctor's office, the hospital, the retirement home, and the carpool lane.)

Luke 24:13-35 New Living Translation (NLT)

The Walk to Emmaus

[13] That same day two of Jesus' followers were walking to the village of Emmaus, seven miles[a] from Jerusalem. [14] As they walked along they were talking about everything that had happened. [15] As they talked and discussed these things, Jesus himself suddenly came and began walking with them. [16] But God kept them from recognizing him.

[17] He asked them, "What are you discussing so intently as you walk along?"

They stopped short; sadness written across their faces. [18] Then one of them, Cleopas, replied, "You must be the only person in Jerusalem who hasn't heard about all the things that have happened there the last few days."

[19] "What things?" Jesus asked.

"The things that happened to Jesus, the man from Nazareth," they said. "He was a prophet who did powerful miracles, and he was a mighty teacher in the eyes of God and all the people. [20] But our leading priests and other religious leaders handed him over to be condemned to death, and they crucified him. [21] We had hoped he was the Messiah who had come to rescue Israel. This all happened three days ago.

²² "Then some women from our group of his followers were at his tomb early this morning, and they came back with an amazing report.

²³ They said his body was missing, and they had seen angels who told them Jesus is alive! ²⁴ Some of our men ran out to see, and sure enough, his body was gone, just as the women had said."

²⁵ Then Jesus said to them, "You foolish people! You find it so hard to believe all that the prophets wrote in the Scriptures. ²⁶ Wasn't it clearly predicted that the Messiah would have to suffer all these things before entering his glory?" ²⁷ Then Jesus took them through the writings of Moses and all the prophets, explaining from all the Scriptures the things concerning himself.

²⁸ By this time they were nearing Emmaus and the end of their journey. Jesus acted as if he were going on, ²⁹ but they begged him, "Stay the night with us, since it is getting late." So, he went home with them. ³⁰ As they sat down to eat, [b] he took the bread and blessed it. Then he broke it and gave it to them. ³¹ Suddenly, their eyes were opened, and they recognized him. And at that moment he disappeared!

³² They said to each other, "Didn't our hearts burn within us as he talked with us on the road and explained the Scriptures to us?" ³³ And within the hour they were on their way back to Jerusalem. There they found the eleven disciples and the others who had gathered with them, ³⁴ who said, "The Lord has really risen! He appeared to Peter. [c]"

1. When you read the Biblical story of Jesus walking on the Emmaus road, what parts of the story might help interpret the story of the coach on the soccer field? How?

2. What have been the unexpected turns of events in your life? In your family's life?

3. How has Jesus appeared to you?

4. What are two to three things you might do in response to the above story and Scripture?

Prayer

Dear God, help me to receive your peace and share your love with the people I meet today. Open my eyes to notice you at work in the lives of those around me. Guide me and give me the courage to do the things you want me to do.

Amen

Chapter 2
This Light in Your Home

By Norm Gordon

Prayer of Invitation

*Gracious God, thank you for making it possible for
me to be with you today. Thank you for never leaving
me nor forsaking me.
I invite you to speak to me a word that transforms me.
I invite you to touch within me a spot that needs to be
healed.
I invite you to move me to do the things that you want
done in our world.
Use this time to get me ready for whatever is coming
next.
Amen*

I left full-time ministry because I knew there were people out there
in the community who were spiritually hungry but who might never
get to church. One way to meet these folks was to host game nights
at our home. So, three or four times a year we invite friends over,
especially our kids' friends and their families. At the beginning of
the evening we gather everyone together. We introduce each person,
say a blessing for our potluck meal, and then spend the rest of the
night playing board or card games. After several successful game
nights, I began to wonder how effective they were since, despite my
efforts to initiate them, no deeper spiritual conversations were
emerging. A good example was Gene and Roberta. They brought

their daughter, Janelle (my own daughter's best friend), to every game night, presumably so the two girls could spend time together. They seemed to enjoy the evenings a lot, connected with us, and felt accepted and loved. However, they would never open up or share anything on a deeper level nor did they invite us to any of their own events.

Last year, we hosted our annual Christmas party, by far the most successful of our game night occasions each year. We had about fifty people. A big potluck meal, complete with turkey and gravy, was followed by silly Christmas games like, using red construction paper and cotton balls, seeing which intergenerational group could dress up one of their members with the best Santa outfit. We finished with a sing-along including both sacred and secular songs, from "Rudolph the Red-Nosed Reindeer" to "Silent Night." It was a blast, but the next morning, after picking up dirty paper plates and restacking folding chairs, I asked myself the same questions: Am I accomplishing my goal? Am I creating a spiritual community or am I just creating a good time for the neighborhood?

This all changed with a letter. One of the families that had been attending—a highly churched, very devout Mormon family—had an eighteen-year-old computer geek son. On January 1, I received a handwritten letter from him. He wrote:

> *I want to thank you for inviting my family to your Christmas party. Every year I go to many Christmas parties in various places for different groups or organizations. Of all of them, your party stands out. I kept thinking about why. When I am at your house and with your family, I feel happier and I sense a presence of light that dwells in your home. It brings people closer together, allows people to talk to one another, and brings peace. In my church they call this*

"the Spirit of God." It is also called "the Light of Christ." I believe you and your family have this light in your home because you are being good examples of Christ. You mentioned to me that you are currently on a quest to help people in the community find religion and God. Keep it up.

Those three final words hit me as if straight from the mouth of God. We decided to continue hosting these events at our house. Before the next scheduled game night, Gene and Roberta said that their daughter Janelle had a soccer game that night and would not be able to attend. We thought that meant that Gene and Roberta would consequently not make it, but much to our surprise, they still showed up, even without their daughter. Others are doing the same—coming consistently, even though the others who come are not necessarily in their friendship circles. As far as a spiritual community, we're still not sure what is emerging, or when it will emerge, but now we have confidence that we're on the right path. We will do our best to host the Light of Christ in our home and trust that God knows best what such a community is supposed to look like.

1. What was Norm's vision?
   What is your vision? Share as much as you know of your vision at this time.

2. What discouraged Norm from his vision? What has discouraged you from your vision?

3. What has encouraged you to remain committed to your vision? How was that the same or different from what encouraged Norm?

John 1:4-5, 9ff
The Word gave life to everything that was created,
  and his life brought light to everyone.
⁵ The light shines in the darkness,
  and the darkness can never extinguish it. *[b]*

⁹The one who is the true light, who gives light to everyone,
was coming into the world....to all who believed him and
accepted him, he gave the right to become children of God.

1. How would you describe "the true light" described in this Scripture passage? How was Jesus light? What was light about Jesus?

2. How did humans experience the "the true light?" How did humans react to the birth and life of Jesus?

3. In what ways, if any, have you experienced "the true light"?

4. How have you responded to "the true light"?

5. What are two or three "next steps" that you would like to explore?

Prayer

God, help me to know whom you have called me to love.
Help me to point to the light of life today. Encourage my
heart today. Help me to persevere.

Amen.

Chapter 3
When All Else Fails, Have A Margarita
By Beth Smith

Prayer of Invitation

*Gracious God, thank you for making it possible for
me to be with you today. Thank you for never leaving
me nor forsaking me.
I invite you to speak to me a word that transforms me.
I invite you to touch within me a spot that needs to be
healed.
I invite you to move me to do the things that you want
done in our world.
Use this time to get me ready for whatever is coming
next.
Amen*

After receiving the text messages of, "Sorry can't make it," "I'm too tired today," "Can't go," and "Not this time," I wasn't sure if I was being blown off, or if my friend just didn't want to hang out with me. It was hard, but I was trying not to take it personally. This was my first invitation to my friend from the neighborhood to join me for a Bible study in our home, and it wasn't getting off to a good start.

I couldn't understand why my friend didn't want to come to our Bible study. We'd known each other for six years and had a friendship where we talked regularly about life struggles. We were studying the book of Psalms, and I felt after all she had gone through, she would really get a lot out of our study, with all the emotional ups and downs of the poetry. My friend had just learned that her husband had cheated on her. And after a messy separation, she was struggling with the reality of raising her four kids alone.

Since my friend wasn't interested in a Bible study, I invited her to join me on a hike with other Christian friends, to be less intimidating. I was hoping she could meet some people who love Jesus and would love her too. She said no. I asked her to join me at church, to meet some of my friends who had helped me through hard times, but she kindly declined. I was struggling with knowing how to help her, and how to create a Christian community to support her during this very difficult and lonely time.

It seemed like all these invitations were too much for her. It didn't feel natural or organic.

I was ready to give up, until one late Friday afternoon, when all the kids of the neighborhood, including hers and mine, were out running around. I decided to start juicing some limes to make margaritas.

I was working with about six limes, and the juice was abundant. I made two glasses with ice and texted my friend that I had a freshly squeezed margarita for her, asking if she would want to come over. She responded "YES," and was at my house in less than five minutes. This was the fastest response I had ever received from her.

We sat on my front porch in the late afternoon September heat. We started with chit-chat about our week and issues at our local school. We had sat on my front porch before, but this day was different. She opened up about her struggles and pain, reasons she didn't go to church, ways she believed in God, and how she desired to know God better. In the safe space we had created together, I told her about my own disappointments and relational struggles. Through this conversation, I gained a wider perspective through which to see my own struggles. She confessed areas of her life that were "really hard" and how she wanted to be a better mom. We listened to one another, we cried—our hearts were raw.

We spent about two hours together, and I sensed the presence of God because at the end of the conversation she felt like "she could do it." She said she could face whatever she had coming her way because she was gaining a bigger perspective and was recognizing God at work in her circumstances. I felt the same way: I had a new mindset for looking at a problem I was having with my co-worker. She helped me to see my situation differently, giving me ways I could listen better. She told me that raising her kids alone was going to be hard, but after our time together over margaritas, she said she had some renewed strength and hope for her life and was ready to keep going. We helped each other that day. Perhaps God helped us too, right there on my front porch with a margarita.

1. What were all the ways that Beth tried to invite her friend to move towards help before inviting her to have a margarita?

2. What do you think were the reasons that her friend declined so many invitations?

3. What might have happened if her friend had said yes to one of the earlier invitations? Would it have been positive? Negative?

4. What were the advantages of meeting her friend on her front porch over margaritas? What could happen on the porch that might not happen as easily at a church or Bible study?

5. What do you think Beth learned through this process?

6. What did you learn from this story?

Acts 10:11-36

Peter fell into a trance. *11* *He saw the sky open, and
something like a large sheet was let down by its four corners.*
12 *In the sheet were all sorts of animals, reptiles, and birds.*
13 *Then a voice said to him, "Get up, Peter; kill and eat
them."*

14 *"No, Lord," Peter declared. "I have never eaten anything
that our Jewish laws have declared impure and unclean."*

15 *But the voice spoke again: "Do not call something unclean
if God has made it clean."* *16* *The same vision was repeated
three times. Then the sheet was suddenly pulled up to heaven.*

17 *Peter was very perplexed. What could the vision mean?
Just then the men sent by Cornelius found Simon's house....*

24 *They arrived in Caesarea the following day. Cornelius was
waiting for them and had called together his relatives and
close friends....*

28 *Peter told them, "You know it is against our laws for a
Jewish man to enter a Gentile home like this or to associate
with you. But God has shown me that I should no longer
think of anyone as impure or unclean....*

34 *Then Peter replied, "I see very clearly that God shows no
favoritism.* *35* *In every nation he accepts those who fear him
and do what is right.* *36* *This is the message of Good News for*

the people of Israel—that there is peace with God through Jesus Christ, who is Lord of all.

1. What made it so significant that Peter went to the home of Cornelius?

2. What could happen at the home of Cornelius that could not have happened at the temple or the synagogue?

3. What did Peter learn in this story?

4. What did Cornelius and his family learn in this story?

5. What can we learn through this story?

6. Who are the people today that do not feel welcome in our congregations?

7. What would be a next step for you if you were to respond to this story and Scripture in your own life?

8. What are two or three next steps that you would like to explore in your life?

Chapter 4
Rediscovering Faith
By A Bridges Disciple as told to Norm Gordon

Prayer of Invitation

*Gracious God, thank you for making it possible for
me to be with you today. Thank you for never leaving
me nor forsaking me.
I invite you to speak to me a word that transforms me.
I invite you to touch within me a spot that needs to be
healed.
I invite you to move me to do the things that you want
done in our world.
Use this time to get me ready for whatever is coming
next.
Amen*

*Trust in the Lord with all your heart and lean not on
your own understanding; in all your ways
acknowledge him, and he will make your paths
straight. (Proverbs 3:5-6)*

I grew up with a religious mother and family. We went to church
most Sundays. I remember going to Vacation Bible School—all of
those traditional things. I was quite spiritual and had always believed
in God. I felt that God was in my life from a young age. However,
as I got older, I began questioning more and more, probably as a
result of what many young people go through. I felt the most
unsettled with my faith during my first years away from home. I
seemed to wander towards the wrong people when I sought answers.

And even when I wandered towards people who were more likely to point me in the right direction, I didn't want to accept their directions. For example, I started attending a Bible study to search for answers, and I asked questions in a way that wasn't welcomed. I was actually asked to leave! Experiences like that kept me away from church for a long while.

It wasn't until my daughter was born that I started to realize again how important faith was. Becoming a mother was an affirmation of God's truth, love, and power. I started looking for a church home. I visited many churches over the years. I even attended a few churches for several months, but none felt like a good fit for me. Regardless, my journey wasn't really about finding a church, although that was an obstacle for me. Rather, it was about finding my way back to fellowship.

After much searching, I couldn't find a place of worship. Churches felt too large, conservative, sterile, or unwelcoming. I couldn't find a place that I was excited to visit each week. I had resigned myself and my children to a mostly secular lifestyle since I was unable to find a church. I wanted to find a church home, but I wanted it to be a good fit. When I wasn't successful after many years of visiting churches, I moved on and let it go. I convinced myself that sending my children to a Christian preschool would provide them with the Sunday school teachings I had enjoyed when I was young. I was content with our life and that I was raising good kids.

What happened next for me was another example of God working in my life.

My husband was asked by a good friend and colleague to join a group he belonged to. He described it to me as a book club that studied the Bible, asked questions, and socialized. It was quite out of character for my husband to be interested in something like this—He had never felt he was missing out by not attending church. His interest in Norm's "book club" was the first blessing! I was hooked from our first meeting. The "book club" was Norm's discipleship group. I had forgotten how nice it was to pray with others. I hadn't seen my children pray with others and talk about what they were thankful for in their lives. I hadn't sung praise in a while… It was a great feeling. Being in the group reminded me of fellowship, and although we didn't directly speak about these things—talking about God, meeting with others, and asking questions—it all helped me realize how important finding a church home was for me and my family. Through the weeks and seasons that followed, faith became important for me again. I discovered that it wasn't acceptable in my own heart to stay away from regular worship.

I began looking again for a church home. It wasn't that I'd found one, but rather the group had led me back to a search. Maybe it opened my heart to a church I would have otherwise closed my mind to. I'm not sure. I'm still on my journey. I'm so glad that the Bridges discipleship was one of the roads God put me on. It has meant the world to me to find new friends and a renewed commitment to my faith.

1. What has led or is currently leading you away from the path of seeking God and fellowship with God's people?

2. What has God done in your life that helped you to discover God anew or to turn back towards God?

3. When you consider the people in your life that don't go to a church regularly, what do you think pushes them away from worship with believers? What do you think might push them towards attending a church and worshipping God?

SCRIPTURE

And so, dear brothers and sisters, we can boldly enter heaven's Most Holy Place because of the blood of Jesus. [20] By his death, Jesus opened a new and life-giving way through the curtain into the Most Holy Place. [21] And since we have a great High Priest who rules over God's house, [22] let us go right into the presence of God with sincere hearts fully trusting him. For our guilty consciences have been sprinkled with Christ's blood to make us clean, and our bodies have been washed with pure water.

[23] Let us hold tightly without wavering to the hope we affirm, for God can be trusted to keep his promise. [24] Let us think of ways to motivate one another to acts of love and good works. [25] And let us not neglect our meeting together, as some people do, but encourage one another, especially now that the day of his return is drawing near. (Hebrews 10:19-25)

4. What are the reasons that people might be afraid to enter into a place of worship?

5. What reasons does the author of Hebrews give to enter into a place of worship?

6. What makes you want to attend worship services? Share a story of what has happened to make you want to worship in a group.

7. What makes you want to avoid worship services? Share a story of what happened that makes you want to avoid worshipping with a group.

8. What might be a next step for you in response to reading this story and the story of Scripture?

Prayer

Almighty Creator, thank you for creating a way for all the many different types of people to be in relationship with you. Thank you for what you have done on the cross to take away our guilt and remove our shame. Thank you for displaying your love and acceptance through the birth, life, ministry, death, and resurrection of Jesus.

I have to admit, God, that there have been times when your presence feels awkward, condemning, and even scary to me. Help me to enter into your presence completely free of any fear, guilt or shame. Help me to overcome every resistance within myself to draw near to you. Help me to enjoy fellowship. Grant me increasing confidence and the power to not only be in your presence but also to help others experience the joy of your presence.

Amen.

Chapter 5
For Those Who Live in Another World
By Rick Ridgway

Prayer of Invitation

*Gracious God, thank you for making it possible for
me to be with you today. Thank you for never leaving
me nor forsaking me.
I invite you to speak to me a word that transforms me.
I invite you to touch within me a spot that needs to be
healed.
I invite you to move me to do the things that you want
done in our world.
Use this time to get me ready for whatever is coming
next.
Amen*

This is a book about storytelling, so I will tell a story about people
who love stories.

Years ago, I started working for a movie studio. I had majored in
English in college and was naïve enough to think that storytelling
had something to do with making movies. It does to a degree for
certain people, but most of the jobs there are mundane. It is more
about moving paper around, and the activities of a large business.

The first day there I started where most people do: in the
entertainment legend, the mailroom. Yup, sorting letters and taking
them around. There I met a fellow named Jon Charles Trapnell.
Jovial, a friend to all, about 5'10", goatee, balding on top. Jon knew

everyone, had a smile for everyone, and could talk your ear off. At first, we would talk about sci-fi stuff, Star Trek in particular.

Jon had an encyclopedic knowledge of movies, The Man from UNCLE, James Bond, comic books, and guns. As for the guns, short story… Jon once applied to be a security guard at the studio. The aptitude test came back and was reported nationwide. Next thing, the Secret Service contacted him and offered him a job protecting the President. His response? "As much as I like shooting at the firing range, I am certain I could never aim a weapon at another human being." And with that, he demurred.

Two decades passed, and Jon and I remained friends. Eventually, I was invited to meet with him and a group of his friends at a local café on Thursday nights at 7:00p.m. Jon named our group "The Knuckleheads" after the Three Stooges. The group included animators, superfans, and friends. The animators had worked in the field for years and years and had been awarded several Emmys. Any given week, four to ten of us gathered, swapped stories of celebrities we'd met, and discussed movies and TV shows. We would discuss politics and religion sometimes, but not often.

During meals, Jon would order things like eggs benedict and, as I said, he could talk your ear off, even while eating. He did tend to spray—by eating while talking—which led to merciless teasing on the part of Harry, an artist who drew famous cartoon characters on merchandise and for theme parks.

After the meals, Jon and I, along with one or two others, would go out in the parking lot and talk for another couple of hours. I had been attending the group for a while, even after being laid off from the studio. The emotional support this group gave me helped me through that time in my life. It was also at that time I started working for Bridges and learned about how to talk meaningfully about religion with folks.

The idea isn't that you go around with a pamphlet and try to convince people forcefully. Your purpose is to learn their history, who they are, and then offer to help when it is appropriate. The Bridges Way is to be part of the group while focusing on the other people in the group. It's not about you 'saving' anyone, just noticing when it might be a good time for the Lord to act through you.

One night, I decided to start a conversation about the Lord with Jon. Somehow, it just felt like the right time. He hadn't been coming to the group much as of late. We thought maybe he was unhappy with the teasing Harry gave him. First, he gave me a Hallmark ornament showing R2-D2 and C-3PO that he'd bought. Then he told me, "Of course I believe! I always have. Why wouldn't I?" The conversation went well.

I talked to him on Sunday as well, but when the next Thursday rolled around, strangely none of us had heard from him. A couple of us decided to check on him.

His place was a few miles away in a condo complex in Toluca Lake. No one had been allowed in for years. The front door of the building was locked. The hallway outside his condo was dimly lit, and there were Amazon boxes in front of the door.

Knock Knock Knock

"JON, C'MON JON! OPEN UP!"

No answer. We forced open the door.

"OH GOD! JON!! NOOOOO!"

He had probably died on Tuesday. Natural causes, heart failure, sixty-two years old at the time. When the police arrived, they discovered about forty guns which were props and items he had collected because "James Bond had this in some movie," or "this Broom-handled Mauser had a scope put on it and was Han Solo's blaster," and so on.

When we finally located his distant family, they asked a friend to take care of the funeral arrangements. At the funeral were friends from the studio and comic shops, family members, and members of the community-eighty-five strong. The services were at my church, and the pastor gave a rousing fire-and-brimstone sermon, which was appropriate, and I was happy we could give him a Christian service. Even the people who identified as atheists in our group appreciated the nature of the sermon. We buried him at Pierce Brothers Valhalla, which was near Fry's Burbank.

For the music, we opened with "Yoda's Theme" and closed with the original Star Trek theme music. I built and painted a 24" model of the Enterprise to go next to his urn, which was a chess piece-looking gold metal box with a Starfleet logo, and the Bible verse "The Lord loves a cheerful giver" on the bottom.

His marker took six months, as we had to get permission from CBS licensing to put the Enterprise on his gravestone. When you look at it, it is in view of a replica of the space shuttle honoring the Challenger and Columbia tragedies. His final resting place is in the flight path of Burbank airport, which is great because he loved planes.

Two years have passed since that time. I still miss him, but I am glad we sent him off well, and that we did speak of greater things.

Make sure to have the important talks with the people in your life. Not necessarily today but have them while you can.

1. Did John befriend Rick, or did Rick befriend John? Give the reasons for your perspective.

2. What made it possible for Rick to discuss John's relationship with God with him?

3. With whom in your life have you been friends for a long time but do not actually know whether or not they experience a relationship with God? What might make it possible for you and your friend to discuss spiritual things?

4. In scripture, there are many ways to describe the Good News: relationship with God, forgiveness, eternal life, adoption as God's child, reconciliation, freedom from the things that bind us, removal of shame, and more. What might the Good News be for that friend? If you are not sure, how would you find out?

SCRIPTURE

[10] Dear brothers and sisters, [a] the longing of my heart and my prayer to God is for the people of Israel to be saved....

"The message is very close at hand;
it is on your lips and in your heart." [d]

And that message is the very message about faith that we preach: [9] If you openly declare that Jesus is Lord and believe in your heart that God raised him from the dead, you will be saved. [10] For it is by believing in your heart that you are made right with God, and it is by openly declaring your faith that you are saved. [11] As the Scriptures tell us, "Anyone who trusts in him will never be disgraced." [e] [12] Jew and Gentile[f] are the same in this respect. They have the same

Lord, who gives generously to all who call on him. [13] *For "Everyone who calls on the name of the Lord will be saved."* [g]

[14] *But how can they call on him to save them unless they believe in him? And how can they believe in him if they have never heard about him? And how can they hear about him unless someone tells them?* [15] *And how will anyone go and tell them without being sent? That is why the Scriptures say, "How beautiful are the feet of messengers who bring good news!" (Romans 10)*

1. For whom does Paul passionately long to be saved?

2. For whom has God given you a longing? If there is no one, would you be willing to ask God to give you such a longing?

3. How does a person become "saved" according to this Scripture passage?

4. What gets in the way of us being willing to share the Good News?

5. What things might help us to overcome the obstacles we experience in having significant conversations about God with the people we care about?

6. What are two or three "next steps" that you might want to explore in your life?

Prayer

Gracious and Forgiving God, thank you for saving me. Help me to share the Good News with others, especially the people that I have known for a long time. May you reveal yourself to them and to me in new ways.

Amen.

Chapter 6
An "Accidental" Messenger
By Dan Steigerwald

Prayer of Invitation

*Gracious God, thank you for making it possible for
me to be with you today. Thank you for never leaving
me nor forsaking me.
I invite you to speak to me a word that transforms me.
I invite you to touch within me a spot that needs to be
healed.
I invite you to move me to do the things that you want
done in our world.
Use this time to get me ready for whatever is coming
next.
Amen*

Some time ago, I scheduled a coffee meeting to connect with a local
pastor, Ryan, whom I had yet to meet face-to-face. Ryan was part of
a missional training cohort we were running in Portland, and we
were meeting at Papaccino's Coffee so that I could fill him in on the
two recent gatherings he had missed. When I entered Papaccino's
that morning, I immediately spotted my neighbor, Jason, sitting in
the corner reading the paper. Seated next to him was another guy
sipping coffee and texting on his phone. I greeted Jason, and he
cheerily returned the greeting with, "Hi Dan, fancy meeting you here
this morning!"

The young man sitting next to him turned out to be Ryan. He of course picked up on the name association, so he bolted upright, hand outstretched, and said, "Hey, you must be Dan Steigerwald."

I said, "Yes, Ryan, that's right. And this is my neighbor,

Jason."

After a cordial nod to Jason, Ryan sat down, and then Jason said, "So what are you guys getting together to talk about? You're obviously just meeting each other for the first time."

I explained to Jason what Ryan does as a pastor among some of the poorest folks of Longview, WA. I mentioned further that Ryan and I were getting together to talk about how I might help him, and his church, be more effective in serving this group and being an agent for good in his city.

Jason knows I do vocational coaching, and he saw that we were ready to get down to business. So, he smiled, nodded his head, and then picked up his paper and pretended read—though I knew he was in earshot of everything we were about to process... and he was listening.

Ryan and I jumped in and talked about the state of American society, including both the bad and the good in terms of how the church tends to relate to culture. To Ryan's credit, he didn't resort to religious, churchy language as pastors sometimes do. We started engaging in a passionate back-and-forth exchange about what's missing in the church's equipping, and how the Good News often gets masked when churches mostly focus on providing religious goods and services to their members. Knowing that Jason is an intellectual, and is big on the idea of meta-narratives, I spoke with some volume about Christ's story and our need as Christians to be true to our story. I also mentioned our need to be interactive in no-strings-attached servanthood with our local neighborhoods and social service organizations.

Ryan piped in some comments about teaching people to do evangelism in ways that seek friendship and not simply letting people know that they need to stop sinning and be morally upright so they can get to heaven.

We talked robustly about such things, and about what the missional training cohort Ryan was about to start involves. I pulled out three books I intended to pass on to Ryan and explained why we chose to use these particular books, noting out of the corner of my eye that Jason was peeking and clearly following the conversation. On and on this went, for forty-five minutes, when Jason suddenly stood up and announced that he needed to get going. While throwing his jacket on, he looked at Ryan and me, and said, "Well, it sounds like a superb process you guys have got in mind to get at those three themes of cultural shifts, sustainability, and leadership." Jason clearly had been listening behind that newspaper, but he was even taking mental notes! And then this sweet ending to our little neighborhood encounter occurred...

Jason said, "Well, I'm not part of any particular sect myself, just trying to be part of the greater good." And I interjected without pause, "I think it is great that you are not part of a sect. Jason, you're part of the tribe of the Pax Americana. We're all part of bigger stories, and we interact with each other and our cities for the common good... Sects don't do that."

Jason then said, "Hmmm, I guess you're more like a tribe than a sect. Then I'm just part of the bigger tribe that wants to find common ground for many different tribes to work together."

"Jason, this is a big part of why we're offering the training Ryan and I are talking about today... it's because we believe that too, just like you." Jason then gave us a big white-toothed grin and headed out the door.

I appreciated the Spirit's work in this encounter. For one, this was the best way for my dear neighbor, Jason, to hear more about what I stand for, including my stance on Jesus, the church, and the gospel. Because Ryan and I had a scheduled meeting, Jason knew it was not appropriate for him to be his usual talkative self. He was bracketed by circumstances into the role of a listener, and I think he heard more in forty-five minutes while fake reading his paper than I could have hoped for in any prolonged, direct conversation with him over the backyard fence.

Secondly, this encounter provided an object lesson for Ryan and me to dissect after Jason left. In short, I could bring Ryan up to speed on what he missed in the last two training gatherings by relating that material to the experience we just had with Jason. The Spirit helped create a teaching moment, and I could see that Ryan was really "getting it" in the fullest extent.

This was a surprising, superb coincidence of lives and stories that I wasn't expecting that morning, and I went away on my bike smiling and thanking God!

I was thinking, "Never underestimate what God is already up to when you walk into a coffee shop…"

1. What makes Dan think that the Holy Spirit was at work in the coffee shop with his friends Ryan and Jason?

2. What experience have you had in your everyday life in which you believe that the Holy Spirit was at work? Share that experience or write it here.

3. What was God already doing in Ryan's life? What was God already doing in Jason's life? What is God already doing in one of your friend's lives?

SCRIPTURE

Therefore, my dear brothers, stand firm. Let nothing move you. Always give yourselves fully to the work of the Lord, because you know that your labor in the Lord is not in vain. (1 Corinthians 15:58)

[13] *Now, who will want to harm you if you are eager to do good?* [14] *But even if you suffer for doing what is right, God will reward you for it. So, don't worry or be afraid of their threats.* [15] *Instead, you must worship Christ as Lord of your life. And if someone asks about your hope as a believer, always be ready to explain it.* [16] *But do this in a gentle and respectful way.* [c] *Keep your conscience clear. Then if people speak against you, they will be ashamed when they see what a good life you live because you belong to Christ.* [17] *Remember, it is better to suffer for doing good, if that is what God wants, than to suffer for doing wrong! (1 Peter 3:13-17)*

1. Describe what you think it means to "[a] always give [yourself] fully to the work of the Lord."

2. What do you think it means to "always be ready to explain [the hope that is within you]"? How would you describe that hope within you?

3. Describe a time when you were able to listen to and share the hope of the Good News with someone from your everyday life. How did you see the Spirit of God at work? If you can't

remember a time, what do you think gets in the way of you having that type of experience?

4. What next step might God be inviting you to take as a result of this time reading the story and Scripture?

Prayer

God, thank you for the hope you have given us. Help me to be ready today to share the Good News and hope with someone you bring my way.

Amen.

Chapter 7
Willing to Try Anything: Even God
By Jim Milley

Prayer of Invitation

*Gracious God, thank you for making it possible for
me to be with you today. Thank you for never leaving
me nor forsaking me.*
I invite you to speak to me a word that transforms me.
*I invite you to touch within me a spot that needs to be
healed.*
*I invite you to move me to do the things that you want
done in our world.*
*Use this time to get me ready for whatever is coming
next.*
Amen

The sun was shining. It was too hot to stand outside. I looked at my watch. The technician was just hooking up the car to the system for smog checks. Across the street I could see the sign that had bothered me for years. "Bad Credit? No Problem. Guaranteed Loans. No One Refused!" I had often thought about talking to the owner about that sign. I felt the nudge, walked to the corner, and pushed the button for the light.

"Is the owner here?" I asked.

"I'm the only one here today," replied an Armenian man in his 50's. We exchanged names.

"Armand," he said. "Can I help you with a car?"

"I'm afraid I'm not buying. I already have two cars. I was just going to ask the owner about the sign."

"What do you mean?"

"That sign about credit."

"What about it?"

"Well, it makes me wonder about the integrity of the business. It sounds like he sells cars to people just to repossess them and sell the car again."

"No, no, no. He's really a nice guy. If anything, he lets people take advantage of him too often."

I thought... Wow, I didn't expect that answer. Maybe my perception has been wrong all these years?

"Well, I would take it down because I think it hurts the business. People with good credit see the sign, figure the place isn't a reputable dealer, and move onto the next car lot."

"You might have a good point. I'll pass your thoughts on to the owner," Armand said. "So, what do you do?"

"I guess the best way to describe my occupation is to say I work for God."

"Work for God... Are you a priest?"

"Not exactly. I am a pastor and I used to be a missionary in Africa. Then I was the outreach pastor in a church in La Canada. Now I'm the director of an organization called Bridges."

"What's Bridges?"

"Bridges is an organization dedicated to helping people who are aware of God's love and compassion and who know what a wonderful difference that makes in people's lives. They learn how to share that with others in the most caring, sensitive, and unobtrusive ways."

As I described Bridges, his heart and soul seemed to come alive and open to me.

"I am in a really bad place in life. I am just working here to make some extra money. My wife is divorcing me, and she has slandered my name to the point that my business is going downhill fast. I sell advertising and make commercials. I also sell time on cable networks."

"Wow, that does sound terrible. Both your marriage and your business is falling apart."

"You know, I spent so much energy and time on both. I really tried my hardest. But no matter what I do, things seem to get worse. My daughter doesn't want to talk to me anymore. Her mother has poisoned her against me."

"Armand, I hear how agonizing and frustrating it is. You have worked hard and long on building up your family and your business. But despite all that energy and focus, both are falling apart. May I ask you a question?"

"Sure."

"Would you like to try something different? If putting all your energy into family and work hasn't been effective, would you be willing to put a similar amount of focus, energy, and effort into your spiritual life? Into building a relationship with God?"

"At this point, I am willing to try almost anything."

"Well, what if we met tomorrow for lunch? I would like to share a few basics with you about getting connected with God."

"I would like to learn more about Bridges," Armand said.

The next day Armand was already sitting at a table when I arrived at the Armenian café.

"I've never read anything from the Bible," he said. "But I have been to church a few times. I am Armenian Orthodox."

"Great," I said. "Let's check out a few verses."

My heart filled with joy as we read the text together: John 3:16 and John 14:1-4. I prayed for Armand. It was a beginning… a new beginning.

When I met Armand a few years later, he reflected, "It took the support of family and good friends like you to get me out of that dark place. It's been an awakening spiritual journey."

And by the way, my car passed the smog check.

1. Why did Jim think he was crossing the street?

2. How would you describe the reason God had Jim cross the street?

3. Have you ever had the sense that God was speaking to you to do something? Describe the experience.

4. Has God ever brought someone into your path with whom you had a meaningful spiritual conversation? If so, describe your experience.

Next Paul and Silas traveled through the area of Phrygia and Galatia, because the Holy Spirit had prevented them from preaching the word in the province of Asia at that time. [7] Then coming to the borders of Mysia, they headed north for the province of Bithynia, but again the Spirit of Jesus did not allow them to go there. [8] So instead, they went on through Mysia to the seaport of Troas.

[9] That night Paul had a vision: A man from Macedonia in northern Greece was standing there, pleading with him, "Come over to Macedonia and help us!" [10] So we decided to leave for Macedonia at once, having concluded that God was calling us to preach the Good News there.

[11] We boarded a boat at Troas and sailed straight across to the island of Samothrace, and the next day we landed at Neapolis. [12] From there we reached Philippi, a major city of that district of Macedonia and a Roman colony. And we stayed there several days.

[13] On the Sabbath we went a little way outside the city to a riverbank, where we thought people would be meeting for prayer, and we sat down to speak with some women who had gathered there. [14] One of them was Lydia from Thyatira, a merchant of expensive purple cloth, who worshiped God. As she listened to

us, the Lord opened her heart, and she accepted what Paul was saying. [15] She and her household were baptized, and she asked us to be her guests. "If you agree that I am a true believer in the Lord," she said, "come and stay at my home." And she urged us until we agreed. (Acts 16)

5. What could it mean that "the Holy Spirit had prevented them" and "the Spirit of Jesus would not allow them" in verses 6 and 7?   What might the Scripture be referring to?

6. How would you describe the experience that led the group to believe that God wanted them to go to Macedonia?

7. How had God prepared Lydia and the women for hearing the Good News that Paul and his group shared?

8. What might be the reasons that God sent Paul to meet Lydia and the group of women by the river?

9. What are one or two next steps that you would like to take as you reflect on the above?

Prayer

Dear God, help me to hear your voice whenever and wherever you choose to speak. Help me to care for the people in my path today. May I be ready to give a listening ear and to share a story of your faithfulness.
Amen.

Chapter 8
Loving Young Parents in A New Way
By Susan Fudge

Prayer of Invitation

*Gracious God, thank you for making it possible for
me to be with you today. Thank you for never leaving
me nor forsaking me.*
I invite you to speak to me a word that transforms me.
*I invite you to touch within me a spot that needs to be
healed.*
*I invite you to move me to do the things that you want
done in our world.*
*Use this time to get me ready for whatever is coming
next.*
Amen

A year ago, at Montclair High School, she quietly came into the
room and sat down. As she began to share her story with the strength
and wisdom of having a one-year-old child, she calmly told her story
of pregnancy, deep depression, and homelessness after the baby was
born. She was only sixteen years old then. These events had sent her
into a spiral of drugs. She said, "I missed three months of my baby's
life because of depression and drugs." Her uncle stepped in and
came along side of her. With his support, she stopped using drugs
and pulled out of the depression because she saw that her daughter
needed her. Due to moving from place to place she had attended
several high schools and was far behind in credits to graduate.

Growing Pains volunteers gave her encouragement, support, love, and a safe place to be with other young moms. We also gave her diapers and hygiene items and tried to stay in touch. Once again, because of homelessness, she left the school. Her phone was turned off. Losing contact, we wondered where she might be. One day while shopping at Costco, I saw her along with all five of her family members. Not having a Costco membership card, they had walked in with someone else to take advantage of the air conditioning, free food, and a safe place to be during the day. I was so excited to see her and meet her family, yet my heart broke as I put the pieces together. They were sleeping in an RV at night but had to leave during the day. We parted ways, but I now had another number to contact her. As I walked around, it was clear to me that God had planned this meeting. Again, I was saddened to hear of more heartache and transitions, but now I was unsure of how to help. Should I buy them shoes? What about clothes? I prayed and asked God to show me and help me know what to do. As I left Costco, there they were, sitting in the food court, counting money on the table to buy lunch. I was thankful to have bought diapers for Growing Pains as I realized the answer to my prayer—give diapers for the baby and buy the family lunch.

She said, "I'm embarrassed!"

I said, "I know, but I have needed help before too—it's hard to receive it."

Since then, we have seen her back at school. She and her family are living in a shelter and are safe. We have provided her with more hygiene items and diapers and given her a card to buy food.

Without your prayers and financial support, we could not have filled these needs for her and her family. Thank you. God sees the broken-hearted, the poor, and the destitute. He provides through us! Thank you in the loving name of Jesus.

Growing Pains was birthed from a desire to reach out to and provide support for pregnant teens. From an after-school program in a local alternative high school at the beginning, to today's groups in four locations, our mission has remained the same—to physically and emotionally bring God's love and acceptance to these young people, to meet their needs as best we can, and to help cultivate their desire to be the best parents they can be for their children.

While our core mission has not changed, it has grown bigger. We have girls who first came while either pregnant or with newborn babies, and they now have kids in school. Yet they continue to come because they recognize Growing Pains as their support group. They also often find themselves reaching out to new girls to offer help and support just as they received it when first coming.

A few years ago, one of the girls asked if her boyfriend could come to the group. That led to our having classes for the boyfriends/dads, as well as for the girls. Most of the males who come eventually share how, growing up, they had either a negative father figure or none at all. They realize that they don't want to raise their own child the same way.

Growing Pains operates as a faith-based ministry that reaches not only young parents, but sometimes even our volunteers. Many of our volunteers come from local churches, but others have heard of our program and ask to be a part of it. We have a beautiful Hindu grandmother who comes to hold the babies during class time. Others come from various faith traditions, or none at all, and they all are touched in some way as they see God working in the lives of our young parents.

Growing Pains Mission Statement is the following:

Growing Pains provides a safe and loving place for teen/young parents to grow and experience the grace of God right where they are.

The stories are too many to tell but one recent story stands out to me. We met a new girl at Montclair High School at a Tuesday group. She is three months pregnant and was kicked out of her home by her grandfather when he found out she was pregnant, forcing her to move in with her boyfriend. She (Summer) called 211 to find out about getting some food and clothing. She was directed to go to a nearby family shelter, so she rode her bicycle from Montclair to Upland, but got nothing after missing the time slot. She called me (Susan) because it was getting dark and her phone didn't have GPS. I called one of our older Growing Pains girls, Krystal, to see if she could pick her up and take her home. Krystal's response to me was, "I'm on my way to get her." She got Summer safely home and we had a quick debriefing conversation. The next day, Summer called me asking for food. My husband went with me to the house, where she and her boyfriend live in a room that they must enter through a window. I was able to talk to her and her boyfriend and provide them with a $50 gift card for food. My heart broke for her.

God has called us to walk beside and love these precious ones. Not judging, but loving them, providing food and necessary items that I/we take for granted. I was left feeling as if I were in a third world country, giving hope to the lost and misfits of our world.

1. What basic needs do Susan and her Growing Pains volunteers meet for young parents?

2. What basic needs do you see in your everyday path? Who are the people who have basic needs that you encounter face to face?

3. How has God met your basic needs?

4. What might be a way for you to meet some basic needs of the people in your daily path?

SCRIPTURE

"Then the King will say to those on his right, 'Come, you who are blessed by my Father, inherit the Kingdom prepared for you from the creation of the world. For I was hungry, and you fed me. I was thirsty, and you gave me a drink. I was a stranger, and you invited me into your home. I was naked, and you gave me clothing. I was sick, and you cared for me. I was in prison, and you visited me.'"[1]

(Matthew 24:34-36)

1. How does the above scripture relate to one or more of the stories about the people in the ministry of Growing Pains?

2. Share a story of how you or someone else has reacted to a stranger that is naked, hungry, thirsty, or in prison—or some partial combination of these things.

---

[1] While many scholars have approached this scripture passage as applying to relationships with all people who have any one or more of the conditions that Jesus lists, some scholars have seen in this passage a reference to the early Christian missionaries who experienced all these conditions *simultaneously* as victims of state-sponsored or religiously motivated persecution. How would this shift of perspective affect your understanding and application of this passage in your life?

3. What could you do to help yourself and others become more comfortable with people in desperate need?

4. What are two or three next steps that you would like to explore in your life?

Prayer

Dear God, help me to notice you in my everyday life. And help me to notice how you are at work in peoples' lives. If there is any way that I could be helpful to your purposes, please guide me in that path.

Amen.

Chapter 9
Building Bridges
By Ed Carlson

Prayer of Invitation

*Gracious God, thank you for making it possible for
me to be with you today. Thank you for never leaving
me nor forsaking me.
I invite you to speak to me a word that transforms me.
I invite you to touch within me a spot that needs to be
healed.
I invite you to move me to do the things that you want
done in our world.
Use this time to get me ready for whatever is coming
next.
Amen*

The United Way of Ottawa County (Ohio) called me and asked, "Do you want to open a non-profit, community café?"

I responded immediately, "Let's talk."

While I didn't know what a "community café" was, I felt that our church's New Beginnings Task Force (NBTF) would be open to exploring the possibility. The NBTF was charged with coming up with a new vision for outreach to our community—we wanted to join God in his work in the neighborhood. I went online to learn more about community cafés—non-profit restaurants that provide free meals to feed insecure people in exchange for volunteering there. Additionally, they try to build bridges in the community, bringing the whole community together to share a meal.

I called two other members of our task force and invited them to join me at a meeting with our county's United Way Executive Director and the owner of a building that had an empty deli space. After an hour of conversation, we were so energized! It felt like this opportunity was an answer to our prayers for clarity in how we should reach out to our community. We committed to moving forward.

We knew we needed to find some professional help. None of us had any restaurant experience, and we needed to involve people from other churches if we were going to pull this off. Our church of seventy-five members, with an average age around seventy, would need help, and we preferred the venture to be ecumenical in nature.

We reached out to the Executive Chef of Our Neighbors Eat (ONE) Bistro, a community café that had been operating for nearly five years. On our visit, we had delicious food and talked with Chef Robert, his staff, and some volunteers. We learned a few things: currently about 40% of their meals were free meals, there had been four baptisms as a result of their café ministry, and they had helped two people start up small businesses. They were clearly making a difference.

We invited our whole community, with a particular push for pastors, to learn about our intent to open a non-profit community café, and to give them the opportunity to join us. Chef Robert was our guest speaker—he wowed them, and a number of people came forward… some to join our steering committee, some to spread the word, and some to serve in various other capacities.

We agreed on our mission: to increase food security and offer all neighbors a place to eat and come together as one community.

Our operating model included:

1. If you can't afford to pay for your meal you are encouraged to volunteer an hour in the restaurant. We wanted to give a hand-up, not a hand-out.

2. If you can afford to pay, you are encouraged to pay a little more, to "pay it forward," to help cover the cost of the free meals.

3. Our staff would be minimal, and the hostess and wait staff would all be volunteers.

4. Our food would be fresh and locally sourced as much as possible.

We found a local food service professional, Stacy, who agreed to serve on our steering committee. She helped with decisions about our menu, equipment needs, staffing, etc. She helped us hire a chef, and then fire the chef when she proved to be very unreliable. We were within three weeks of our planned opening date with no chef when I received a call from Stacy. She said God had really been working on her, she felt very committed to our mission, and she wanted to work with us full-time. We were delighted! Our prayers had been answered!

People ask us how we came up with our name, Bistro 163 (www.bistro163.org). We tell them we are right off State Highway 163, which runs the length of our county, and we recite Proverbs 16:3—roughly translated as "Entrust your plans with the Lord and they will be successful."

We have been open for nineteen months and have served nearly 28,000 meals, including about 7,000 free meals. We are only open for lunch, 11 to 2 six days a week. However, we have a free community dinner once a month. everyone is invited (we average around 150), and during the school year we have a weekly Snack and Study program after school for K-8th grade students, many of whom live in subsidized housing nearby.

We have learned a lot over the last two years. As Chef Stacy said, "I hadn't seen the face of hunger before, but now I have." We have been blessed by those to whom we provide free meals. They come for more than the food—they come because they feel accepted as they are, they feel loved, and they value the friendships that have formed. We have been blessed by those who "pay it forward" (over $60,000) and rave about the food, the sense of joy and community, and their thankfulness for our mission and the opportunity to help others. We have been blessed by our many volunteers (sixty+). Their enthusiasm, friendliness, willingness to work extra in a pinch, donation of time and material to build a new counter and handle our maintenance needs, work with the Snack and Study children, and board service. We have been blessed by our staff, many of whom have faced tough times and had limited employment opportunities… for their loyalty, cheerful attitudes, and commitment to our mission.

But most of all we have been blessed by God. He has provided what we needed when we most needed it. He has truly given us reason to entrust our plans with him. We have had many transformative miracles impacting both those served and those serving. God is so faithful!

1. What reasons could Ed have given not to take on this project?

2. What did Ed do that made success more likely?

3. What did Ed and others learn through the process?

4. What projects have you been challenged to take on in life?

5. What did God teach you through your experience of implementing the project?

SCRIPTURE

[22] "When you harvest the crops of your land, do not harvest the grain along the edges of your fields, and do not pick up what the harvesters drop. Leave it for the poor and the foreigners living among you. I am the Lord your God."

If farmers leave the edge of their fields unharvested for the poor, what relational dynamics occur as the poor come to harvest the grain?

How might some of these dynamics relate to the dynamics described in Ed's story of a community café? (Leviticus 23)

SCRIPTURE

[42] For seven days you must live outside in little shelters. All native-born Israelites must live in shelters. [43] This will remind each new generation of Israelites that I made their

ancestors live in shelters when I rescued them from the land
of Egypt. I am the Lord your God." (Leviticus 23)

1. If every family in America had to spend seven days a year living outside in a tent, how might that impact the relationship between those in homes and those who live in tents every night on the streets?

2. How might the relational dynamic that emerges when everyone sleeps in tents for a week relate to the relational dynamics that Ed describes in his story?

3. What are two or three next steps that God might be encouraging you to take?

Prayer

Dear God, thank you for preparing good things for us
to do in this life. Forgive me for when I have walked
away from opportunities which you have provided.
Help me to say yes to your invitations. I acknowledge
that I need your help for so many things in my life and
especially for the special projects that you place
before me. Strengthen my heart, my mind, my hands,
and my feet to do your will.

Amen.

Chapter 10
God's Gift: "My Miraculous, Precarious Journey to Childbirth"
By Deborah Milley

Prayer of Invitation

Gracious God, thank you for making it possible for me to be with you today. Thank you for never leaving me nor forsaking me.
I invite you to speak to me a word that transforms me.
I invite you to touch within me a spot that needs to be healed.
I invite you to move me to do the things that you want done in our world.
Use this time to get me ready for whatever is coming next.
Amen

For I am convinced that neither death nor life, neither angels nor demons, neither the present nor the future, nor any powers, neither height nor depth, nor anything else in all creation, will be able to separate us from the love of God that is in Christ Jesus our Lord. (Romans 8:38-39)

As a young girl I have a memory of my mom asking me what I wanted to be when I grew up. I can hear her chuckles as I responded, "I want to be a plain old mommy just like you!"

I love children and, like Hannah in the Bible who cried out to God for a child, I longed to one day have my own children. Marriage? Great! Have children? Nirvana!

After college, Bible school, church planting in South America, and a seminary degree, I married a like-minded man with a heart for God at the age of 32 and we went off to Ethiopia as missionaries.

Jim and I were thrilled with my first pregnancy, naively telling every human being we met that a "little Milley" would be joining the world in seven short months. During week nine, I started to bleed and cramp. I miscarried. The breath was knocked out of me; a dagger driven into my heart.

Disappointment mounted as the months passed until, one year later, I was pregnant once again. We held our breath until the second trimester when we started to feel the baby's kicks. We then proclaimed to the world our good news! Our hearts were bursting with joyful anticipation.

The pregnancy went smoothly. Daily I talked and sang to our baby, played music and prayed for her. Her kicks in response grew stronger each day. Strong kicks to my ribs and bladder, at times echoed by the guitar when I picked it up to play.

Jim and I returned to the States for our baby's birth. Our church family organized a baby shower and an evening to spend celebrating and opening gifts. I was living on the mountain top.

The morning of our baby's due date, I waddled down to breakfast and waited for the usual "good morning" kicks as I drank my orange juice. No kicks… how strange. All morning I poked at the baby to elicit a kick. All remained still. I didn't want to worry Jim. At the same time, fear was building within me. The doctor's office staff encouraged me to come in, reassuring me that all was fine during my visit the day prior.

Once in the doctor's office, attached to the sonogram, I will never forget the chilling words we heard: "I'm sorry. Your baby has no heartbeat." Shock... disbelief... fear... grief. "This can't be happening to us!"

That night my labor was induced and the next morning Rachel Elizabeth was born, 7 pounds 10 ounces, a tightened knot on her umbilical cord. A "true knot" is the medical term—not uncommon, but rarely the cause of a baby's in-utero death.

In my grief I screamed at God, "Why, God? WE DON'T DESERVE THIS! WHY?"

With heavy hearts and empty arms, we returned to Ethiopia.

For the next six years I continued to serve God, speak the "Christian talk," but I did not forgive God.

At age forty-two, to our joyful amazement, I became pregnant with our son Nathaniel. At five months of pregnancy my doctor wanted to do an amniocentesis because a "soft marker" for Down syndrome was seen in the ultrasound. To the doctor's consternation, I refused, knowing that an amniocentesis posed the risk of premature labor. I knew that this would be my last pregnancy and, regardless of disability, I would love this baby boy.

At week thirty-six I relented and had the testing done. The following day I went into labor—four weeks before the baby's due date. With each contraction the baby went into distress. Because of the baby's small size though, the doctor was able to reach up and unwrap the umbilical cord that was wrapped several times around his neck.

Nathaniel James Milley was born 5 pounds 11 ounces, a healthy baby boy.

After the birth, the doctor told us the cord was wrapped so tightly around the baby's neck that if I had not gone into labor four weeks early, he probably wouldn't have survived. Even the doctor used the word "miracle" to describe Nathan's birth. Shock… disbelief… "God, WE DIDN'T DESERVE THIS MIRACLE! Thank you, Lord! Thank you for your mercy upon us."

I felt my anger towards God melt away. I began to realize that I didn't "deserve" the bad in my life, nor the good.

I don't "deserve" living in the richest nation in the world, nor being born with white skin. I don't "deserve" the years of quality education I received, nor a lifetime of high-quality healthcare.

"God, I will worship you and thank you in ALL of life's circumstances. When I journey through life with sorrow and suffering as my travel companions, when I receive abundant blessings, I will rejoice in you, God, and rest in your loving arms."

My heart now resonates with the words of the prophet Habakuk:

Scripture

"For though the fig tree shall not flourish,

Neither shall fruit be in the vines;

The labor of the olive shall fail,

And the fields shall yield no food;

The flock shall be cut off from the fold,

And there shall be no herd in the stalls:

"YET... I will rejoice in Jehovah!

I will rejoice in the God of my salvation.

Jehovah, the Lord, is my strength;

And he maketh my feet like hind's feet,

And will make me to walk upon my high places." (Habakuk 3:17-19)

1. What in your life has made you angry at God? Why do you think it made you angry?

2. What has helped you to overcome, move through, or hold differently your anger at God?

3. What are things that help you to pray together with Habakuk through her words?

4. What are things that make you not want to pray with Habakuk through her words?

5. What things could you do that might help you manage your anger with God?

6. In what ways might Debbie's journey with pain and sorrow be used for good in her life today?

7. What do you think God is asking you to do next? Write it here.

Prayer

Dear God, I want to tell you the truth. Sometimes I really hate you. Sometimes I am so angry. There are so many things wrong in this world, and there seems to be so much suffering and pain that really isn't necessary. And yet I know that I cannot see the beginning and the end, nor can I even see all of what is happening today. Your wisdom is beyond my wisdom. Help me to trust you. Help me to live in the hope of a new heaven and a new earth, a time when you will dwell with your people, and every tear will be wiped from our eyes. Come Lord Jesus. We desperately need you.

Chapter 11
Dancing with Fountains
By Jim Milley

Prayer of Invitation

*Gracious God, thank you for making it possible for
me to be with you today. Thank you for never leaving
me nor forsaking me.
I invite you to speak to me a word that transforms me.
I invite you to touch within me a spot that needs to be
healed.
I invite you to move me to do the things that you want
done in our world.
Use this time to get me ready for whatever is coming
next.
Amen*

When I saw the fountain, I could see my little girl Amanda in her
white dress. It had ribbons and lace. The fading light of the setting
sun was sparkling on the water and bouncing off the sequins. She
was looking into the water as if to find a fish or a leaf or a twig—but
this fountain was meticulously maintained. I walked hand-in-hand
with my wife Debbie, making our way around the lattice-covered
path, tracing the curve of the half-moon's arc. I could smell the roses
and several more unfamiliar flowers. Passing by the benches, we
chose instead to sit on top of a pillar on the steps facing the view of
the fountain. It was flanked by towering palms and the outline of the
five-star Sheraton hotel. At that moment, the symphonic music

gushed forth, the water erupted into the sky, and the lights began to dance to the music.

But it wasn't just the lights that danced. Amanda danced. Amanda swirled. Her dress rose and twirled. She swayed side to side. She clapped and shook. She shuddered her shoulders as only Ethiopians can. When the music and the water and the lights finally stopped, a thunderous round of applause erupted as suddenly as had the fountain. Others had been lining the half-moon walkway. They had become participants in the moment of pure innocence and joy. Amanda had been a sole performer for an audience of scores of Ethiopian couples. Yes, our life in Ethiopia had moments of tremendous beauty and joy.

The Ethiopian doctor showed us on the flickering screen that the spine of our baby seemed short for the number of weeks of pregnancy. "I am not that concerned," he said. "We may have mistaken the date of conception." We forgot all about it.

On the plane to America, I couldn't stop telling people that I was going home to become a father again. My daughter was going to be named Sarah.

And then we got the news.

Pastor Don Gruer drove me around in his car. I was talking nonstop: "I don't understand how we could lose Rachel and now have a Down syndrome baby." "I just can't take anymore." "I just don't know how I am going to handle it." "I just don't know what to do." "I do not want to answer any more questions about babies or see any more presents or read any more magazine articles." What I wanted was pizza. And plenty of it.

We pulled into the parking lot. I was in the passenger seat in the front, ready to comfort my soul with an Italian American tradition. And then I saw it. It was a yellow school bus. I watched out the window of the car as the children started to get off the bus to go into the pizza parlor. The first child got off. He looked like he had Down syndrome. And then the second child got off the bus. And she looked like she had Down syndrome too. It took me a while to understand what I was seeing and what had just happened. Every child had Down syndrome. I wasn't dreaming. I had never before seen a bus filled with children with Down syndrome. Why was I seeing this today? Now? At this moment?

A peace came over me. I knew what God was saying: "I have everything under control. You do not have to worry. You do not have to handle this alone. I will help you. Others will help you. I see you. I know you are distressed. I have not forgotten you. I have not abandoned you. You are my child. And your children are my children. All will be well."

When I got back to the house, I went to throw away one of the magazines that shows the perfectly formed, smiling babies on the front cover, with the mother who smiles back at them. As I went to throw away the magazine, it opened "randomly" to the page with an article about Down syndrome babies. Once again, I sensed God saying, "I know the situation that you are in. I am with you. Do not be afraid."

Two years later, the doctor said the word, but it came into my ear as an elongated, distorted, slow-motion sound, like someone had slowed down a tape recorder. Despite my automatic defenses, I heard the word "cancer." Sarah had cancer.

The tubing for the chemo ran into a port that went directly into Sarah's heart. Debbie or I, or someone else, had to watch Sarah 24/7 to make sure she did not pull on the tubing. We had to keep it from tangling. There was a scissors clamp on the wall. That was in case the port to the heart broke and blood began to pour out. In that case, we were to remain calm, take the scissors from the wall, and clamp off the port.

Sarah, at just two years of age, spent over a week in the hospital at least ten times that year. Other days were full of blood and platelet transfusions, doctor's appointments, blood draws, and examinations. So for a whole year, we traveled back and forth to the hospital, following the same path time after time. And on that path, time after time, we passed a fountain. A fountain that reminded me of that magical moment in Ethiopia when Amanda danced in joy, and yet a fountain that now reminded me of the attack of illness, an attack on the joy of the dance.

Five years of annually walking by the fountain went by. Ten years went by. Now Sarah says, "I want to go to college." "I want to go to Paris with Amanda." "I want to get a job." These are Sarah's aspirations today. She is seventeen years old, loves to dance, and spends hours each day singing. I spend more time worrying today about what she can do than what she can't do. And I believe that she is going to dance through a lot of things in life. It's what I believe when I see a fountain.

1. What does the fountain represent?

2. What are the fountains in your life?

3. In what ways did God communicate to Jim in the story?

4. In what ways has God communicated to you during times of struggle or adversity?

SCRIPTURE

[10] *Jesus answered her, "If you knew the gift of God and who it is that asks you for a drink, you would have asked him, and he would have given you living water."*

[11] *"Sir," the woman said, "you have nothing to draw with and the well is deep. Where can you get this living water?* [12] *Are you greater than our father Jacob, who gave us the well and drank from it himself, as did also his sons and his livestock?"*

[13] *Jesus answered, "Everyone who drinks this water will be thirsty again,* [14] *but whoever drinks the water I give them will never thirst. Indeed, the water I give them will become in them a spring of water welling up to eternal life."*

[15] *The woman said to him, "Sir, give me this water so that I won't get thirsty and have to keep coming here to draw water." (John 4:10-15)*

1. What does the constantly flowing, bubbling spring of water represent in this story?

2. In what ways is the woman in the story thirsty? How does she show her thirst?

3. In what ways are you thirsty? How do you show your thirst?

4. In what ways are people in your networks thirsty? How do they show their thirst?

5. How might you experience more of the fountain of living water in your life?

6. How might your friends discover more of the fountain of Jesus in their lives?

7. What are one or two next steps for you in response to your reading and reflection today?

Prayer

Living Water, sometimes I try to act as if I am not thirsty. But you can see the truth. So, I admit it. I get really thirsty. I am thirsty now. I need a deeper relationship with you. Please help me to experience the living water that you spoke about. Give me the strength to do the things that will help me to drink.

And Living Water, I know that there are so many around me who are thirsty. Some are literally dying of thirst. Help me to say and do today the things that will point people towards you.

Amen.

Prayer

I have to admit, God, that there have been times when your presence feels awkward, condemning, and even scary to me. Help me to enter into your presence completely free of any fear, guilt, or shame. Help me to overcome every resistance within myself to draw near to you. Help me to enjoy fellowship. Grant me increasing confidence and the power to not only be in your presence but also to help others experience the joy of your presence.

Amen.

Chapter 12
My Miracle

By Teri Sutherland

Prayer of Invitation

Gracious God, thank you for making it possible for me to be with you today. Thank you for never leaving me nor forsaking me.
I invite you to speak to me a word that transforms me.
I invite you to touch within me a spot that needs to be healed.
I invite you to move me to do the things that you want done in our world.
Use this time to get me ready for whatever is coming next.
Amen

My story begins at age twenty-seven. I had graduated from college with a degree, but I had not found a career and was going from job to job trying to find one. I was struggling financially, and my personal life was also unstable as I was dating a man who did not have the same religious convictions as I did.

I had several jobs after college, from door-to-door insurance sales to working in a gym selling memberships. Finally, I wound up with a job at a national rental car agency. This is where I met the man who would change my life forever.

Mr. Wonderful was twenty years older and did not seem to worry about finances, or much of anything. This was attractive because I worried about everything, especially finances. He seemed to have answers to all my problems and acted like nothing affected him. I saw him as stable and powerful. This was super attractive to an insecure young lady. The only flaw he had was that he was married, but he had assured me that he would get a divorce as soon as his youngest son graduated from high school. After 16 years of enduring our affair, his wife finally filed for divorce. I stayed in the relationship for two more years before I decided to leave.

Why did I stay in the relationship? There were several reasons. The first reason was that I told myself a lot of lies. One of the lies I told myself was, "No man would want to date a woman who had been in an adulterous relationship." Or, "It is better to be with him than to be by myself." Then there was, "Our relationship is better than so and so's relationship."

The other thing I did was isolate myself from others. I lied to most of my friends about the relationship because I knew it was wrong. I was afraid of losing their friendship if I told them the truth. I created an emotional prison by telling myself lies.

One of the biggest lies I told myself was that if I showed him true love he would leave and want to be with me more than his wife. I held my life together pretty well, but I did not see how this relationship was hurting my relationships with my family. I established myself in a career as an educator and even got my master's degree.

Then on January 15, 2005 my world was blown apart… My oldest nephew took his life at the age of twenty-one. This was so emotionally devastating that I could barely function at work. I had to seek professional help and began taking antidepressants to deal with the loss of my nephew and the dysfunctional relationship I had with my boyfriend. I was an emotional mess!

Through counseling, I began to see how unhealthy my relationship was with my boyfriend. I had told myself that, if he had just gotten a divorce, our relationship would have been perfect. However, I learned through counseling that this was not true… as a matter of fact, by the time I started to see a counselor, he had gotten a divorce and our relationship was still a mess! He had no desire to change any of his behaviors, regardless of how they affected me, and I was frustrated and unhappy.

After a year of counseling and trying to fix our relationship I finally decided that I deserved better. I was finally done. He lived in my house, and though he had made verbal agreements several times to leave, he made no effort to do so. After several months of him taking no action, I finally asked my brother to come and help move him out. However, once he moved out, he continued to harass me. He would call me until my answering machine was full, and I had to change my number. He would call my work and come by bringing me gifts so that I would take him back. He even had his ex-wife call me for him. Finally, I'd had had enough. He continued to harass me even after I told him to leave me alone, so I filed a restraining order. When I filed the restraining order, the clerk told me that it was very unlikely that it would be granted, as he hadn't been violent towards me. She was right… the restraining order was denied because the lack of violence.

What happened next was a complete surprise. It was April 15, 2017.

It was after church that I found myself sitting in my car at the nearby donut shop. My ex pulled up alongside me. After we exchanged glances of acknowledgement, he picked up a gun from the passenger seat, pointed it right at me, and pulled the trigger. The first shot severed my vocal cords and shattered my voice box. The second shot hit my door jam, and that was when I decided to back out of the parking space and drive around to the front of the shopping center. I pulled up in front of the grocery store. He followed and continued to shoot at me. The next three bullets grazed my head. Another bullet went through my clothing but missed my torso. I spent the next three and a half weeks in three different hospitals, and the next two and a half months not knowing if I would ever be able to speak again.

By the grace of God, I lived, and my voice returned, but my life would never be the same. That same year, I consider it a "gift" that, on my birthday, the man who had tried to murder me left this world permanently. He had been incarcerated and declared unfit to stand trial. He wound up in a mental hospital, where he died. The gift of his death meant I did not have to go through a trial and relive every moment of the nightmare again and again.

And yet, as odd as it is to say, I am in a better place because of what I went through. I vividly remember thinking I was going to die and had not done enough for God while I was on earth. I felt deep regret. I soon learned God wasn't done with me here, as He has given me a voice and passion to help others who are struggling in similar situations. God has provided many opportunities to share my story, and now I volunteer my time on a regular basis with a teen mom ministry. I had initially thought I had nothing to offer them. However, as I have shared my story with them and walked beside them as a mentor, I have learned that our journeys are very similar. I realize that everyone who struggles with low self-esteem and finds themselves in controlling and abusive relationships needs to be the one to walk away from it... No one else can do it for her. I want to be a voice of encouragement to let them know they actually have a choice and can live a happy life!

1. How would you describe Terry's main problem?

2. What helped Terry to recognize and take action to solve her problem?

3. What situations in your life relate to any part of Terry's story?

4. How did Terry begin to value herself more?

SCRIPTURE

⁹ As Jesus was walking along, he saw a man named Matthew sitting at his tax collector's booth. "Follow me and be my disciple," Jesus said to him. So Matthew got up and followed him.

¹⁰ Later, Matthew invited Jesus and his disciples to his home as dinner guests, along with many tax collectors and other disreputable sinners. ¹¹ But when the Pharisees saw this, they asked his disciples, "Why does your teacher eat with such scum?[c] "

¹² When Jesus heard this, he said, "Healthy people don't need a doctor—sick people do." ¹³ Then he added, "Now go and learn the meaning of this Scripture: 'I want you to show mercy, not offer sacrifices.'[d] For I have come to call not those who think they are righteous, but those who know they are sinners."

1. What relationships do you see between this Scripture passage and Terry's story?

2. Who are the "sinners" in this passage? What did Jesus do for them, according to this passage?

3. Who are the sinners in your networks and neighborhoods?

4. In what ways do you feel like a sinner?

5. What might help you to feel less ashamed of your shortcomings and failings?

6. What are two or three next steps that you would like to explore in your life?

Prayer

Forgiving God, help me to experience your love.
Help me to recognize and feel your love. By your
love, enable me to love others—even the others that I
will meet today.

Amen

Chapter 13
God Talks to Us In Many Ways
By Julia Rodriguez

Prayer of Invitation

*Gracious God, thank you for making it possible for
me to be with you today. Thank you for never leaving
me nor forsaking me.
I invite you to speak to me a word that transforms me.
I invite you to touch within me a spot that needs to be
healed.
I invite you to move me to do the things that you want
done in our world.
Use this time to get me ready for whatever is coming
next.
Amen*

When I was young, I had a recurring dream. Back then I couldn't
understand why it occurred so frequently or what its significance
was. Now that everything has played out and I am able to look back
on those days, I believe this dream was a message from God
preparing me for what was to come.

The dream was about my mother's friend and my dear childhood
companion, Lalo, opening the front door of our apartment revealing
my mother on one side and my sister on the other. Every single time
I had this dream, Lalo would ask the same question, "Cual quieres?",
or "Which one?" Before I even had the chance to reply, I would

abruptly wake up, the warm dream slipping from my eyes, returning me to reality.

I knew that I didn't have the best Mother, but I managed to tolerate her the first six years of my life. The day came, though, when the catalyst to a whole chain of events would arrive. This catalyst had a name—José. He moved in because my mother said he was a close friend. He didn't treat me right, and was constantly touching me inappropriately, despite my pleas for him to stop. So, one day I decided to tell my mother about my situation. She might have been abusive and neglectful, but when it came to something as serious as this, I was sure she'd fix everything. Once I told my mother this information in confidence, she called me the very next day. She had Jose with her, and she called me a liar. She taunted me, saying that José had denied my accusations and that I was a horrible child. I stared at her incredulously. So many thoughts ran through my brain in that moment: What? This isn't supposed to happen! Why would you do this? You're my mother. Mothers are supposed to be nurturing and kind. How could you? At six years old, I was put to shame, right in front of José. My Mother took her friend's words over mine. I wanted her to feel guilty, so I began to cry. I should have known better—such things didn't work on her. She began to laugh, and José joined in. I couldn't take it. I ran to my safe- haven, the upstairs closet, and cried for who knows how long.

I always went there to pray and hoped, yearned, for something better. But this moment helped something click in my head... I'm alone in this. No one can help me now. It took me such a long time to tell my mother of my situation, because somewhere in the back of my mind I knew the outcome—but I had dared to hope. I told no one else. I suffered in silence. I didn't want to be hurt again, so I kept my mouth shut. I was able to handle my mother's reaction, but what if I told Lalo, my dearest person, about my situation and he did the same?

No, I knew I wouldn't be able to handle it. I avoided going home, staying out as late as I could because I knew I wouldn't be able to handle it. I avoided my home because I knew what awaited me there. I even tried falling asleep at a park once, but it got so cold that I eventually had to go back to where I knew José was waiting for me.

One day my sister, who was twenty-one years old at the time and living apart from us, was driving me around on one of her many errands. She said that we could go to her friend's house before she dropped me back off with my mother. We drove by my house quickly and I remembered looking out at the house with different eyes. It looked so gloomy and forbidding. A monster only I could see lurked behind those curtains. Couldn't others see my pain, or did they just not care? That was when I realized I couldn't go back. Anything had to be better than this—living in constant fear in my very own home. The sick feeling I had every time I went home was crippling.

Telling my sister of my situation was an out-of-body experience. I watched myself walk towards her and lean down to whisper in her ear, only a few simple words that altered my life forever. She grabbed my wrist and quickly snatched me back to reality. We went to the police station and she had me tell them my situation. When we came out, I saw Lalo talking to an officer. "Lalo!" I screamed and ran towards him. At first, I thought that my sister had called him to tell him I was there, but my sister explained to me that he had come to file a missing person's report since I had been gone for a long time.

He does care, he loves me, I thought. I was ecstatic. My grandfather was at the police station, showing his concern for me, and my sister trusted my words when my own mother didn't. I was happy for that moment—everything seemed right. But then that moment passed.

My grandfather picked me up and began yelling at my sister because she had never returned home with me. They were bickering and fighting. I didn't understand. Was there something wrong? All we had to do was make the bad guy go away and everything would go back to normal. The police officer came and had my sister take me from Lalo's protective embrace. The officer explained to Lalo that, due to the circumstances, I had to go with my sister... there was nothing he could do. I was excited for a sleepover at my sister's house before I went back home. It felt like a movie. People usually don't look back during those times. That's stupid, I thought. I looked back to wave at Lalo before we left the police station.

His grief-stricken face is still etched in my mind. My seventy-year-old protector, standing there, watching me be taken away—helpless to grab me and protect me and bring me home. Just as I turned around to look ahead, I made a mental note. Never look back from now on. Things are going to be different.

It was difficult for me, at first, to adjust to this new change. Lalo was the one who had showed me all the good in the world. I wasn't even his child, yet he was the one who took me to the park, made sure I was fed, and most importantly, loved me. His genuine kindness has forever changed me and is the reason I try to model my life after his actions. If I can somehow help someone as he helped me, I'll feel like I've returned the favor that I was blessed to experience.

I'm very glad I had that dream to help me during this crisis. Without it, I wouldn't have been able to let my dearest person go and move on with my life. I would have wanted to stay by my precious protector's side and endure any torture, as long as he was there to comfort me and care for me. The dream helped me accept the circumstances and move forward. The choice wasn't really between my sister and my mother... it was between my sister and Lalo. I wouldn't have hesitated for one instant to choose Lalo. This dream helped me see the world through different eyes. Even though I had to grow up a little sooner than others, I'm sure God heard all my prayers from my safe haven in the closet, and was there to guide me through, every step of the way. For always providing me with a protector, I thank Him and I strive to amplify the kindness shown to me in my lifetime to others. This blessed dream, accompanied by this series of events, has helped me grow as a person and continues to affect my outlook on life and aid me in my life goal to spread the kindness shown to me as a child.

1. How did Julia interpret her dream? How do you interpret it?

2. What is Julia saying about God? How do you feel and what do you think about it?

3. Why is this dream important to Julia? In what way did it help her?

SCRIPTURE

Joseph responded, "Both of Pharaoh's dreams mean the same thing. God is telling Pharaoh in advance what he is about to do. ²⁶ The seven healthy cows and the seven healthy heads of grain both represent seven years of prosperity. ²⁷ The seven thin, scrawny cows that came up later and the seven thin heads of grain, withered by the east wind, represent seven years of famine. ²⁸ This will happen just as I have described it, for God has revealed to Pharaoh in advance what he is about to do. (Genesis 41:25-28)

1. How did this dream change the life of Pharaoh? Of Joseph? Of the Egyptians? Of the Jewish People? Of us today?

2. Have you ever had a dream in which God described to you something that was to come? Write out the dream and its interpretation or share the dream verbally with someone you trust.

3. If you have never experienced something like a vision, dream, or word from God, would you like to? If so, pray and ask God to speak to you in dreams, visions, and words of wisdom.

4. What next step is God asking you to take?

Chapter 14
Dreaming or Dreaming

By Mari Barrach

Prayer of Invitation

*Gracious God, thank you for making it possible for
me to be with you today. Thank you for never leaving
me nor forsaking me.
I invite you to speak to me a word that transforms me.
I invite you to touch within me a spot that needs to be
healed.
I invite you to move me to do the things that you want
done in our world.
Use this time to get me ready for whatever is coming
next.
Amen*

*"For I know the plans I have for you," declares the
Lord, "plans to prosper you and not to harm you,
plans to give you hope and a future." (Jeremiah
29:11)*

The year was 1997. The fall breeze carried winds of change and
freedom for the incoming, naïve, soon-to-be freshmen students at
Oral Roberts University (ORU). I should know because I was one of
them. I was a street-smart girl but had high idealistic hopes to make
it in the school of music and find the love of my life before my
junior year.

After receiving my rejection letter from the school of music, I found myself sharing my dismay with a friend. She encouraged me to audition for a scholarship choir. If I made it in, they'd have to let me pursue my dream major. And so, I did. I auditioned and made it in! I wasn't planning on becoming an opera star—I wanted to become a teacher and focus on musical theater and maybe film.

For a while, I rode high on the acceptance letter and small scholarship, but once I realized how far behind I really was, reality set in. I was not a studied musician who came from a large high school with an excellent jazz program. I had big city roots but went to a small private school that did not invest in music programs, and, as a youngster, I also refused to be diligent with the disciplined side of music. So here I was, a musician at heart who longed to be the best but couldn't... a musically illiterate songbird with a lot of catching up to do.

As my freshmen year floated on, so did I. I gave up my fantasy, scraping by without really learning. If I couldn't succeed in one area of my life, maybe I could in the next area... love. Now let me give you a little background idea of where my headspace was with the idea of love:

My high school first kiss—my first boyfriend—cheated on me. I figured it out very quickly—I wasn't a sucker, and I wasn't overly emotional about it. Boom! Right out of the gate, I decided to close the door on serious relationships in high school because I knew my husband wasn't nearby. I was going out of state to school, so he had to be there. Did I mention I was idealistic?

Well, there he was, swarthy, charming... McDreamy! I saw him standing in the dorm lobby... we made eye contact, frozen in time, just like the movies. I wanted him for myself but suddenly another idea came to mind. There was a school event called "roommate-a-date" where you could play matchmaker for your dorm friend for an all-campus dating event. So, I had the idea that maybe my senior roommate wouldn't make my life hell if I could just set her up with a hot man on a fun evening out. I waltzed up to him and introduced myself. He opened the door like a true gentleman, so we could step outside for a quiet conversation. I jumped right into roommate-a-date, and he obliged.

We talked about everything in that moment, from the school of music down to my Lebanese ethnicity. He told me that he was going to marry a woman with Middle Eastern roots because he grew up in Israel. I soon learned about his love of literature and language. The rest was history. He never ended up on roommate-a-date. My roommate still hated me, but I didn't care. I was in bliss... that space where you are floating on a cloud, also known as the honeymoon stage.

Ice skating rinks, dinner, and movies followed. Things were moving quickly, hot and heavy, and I wanted to be clear about the lines... no sex. I was still a virgin and wanted to wait. He was not a virgin and, of course, did his best to care but could not.

Several months later, we ventured out to the Ozarks with a group of friends on spring break. The newfound love of my life was becoming pushy—was it time to reconsider waiting?

Did he care? Would he marry me? I pushed back. The trip was full of waterfalls, mud, rain, and ultimately darkness. We headed to a friend's house when the trip was over, and this time he pushed a little harder and got his way. I was devastated. At the time, I was in denial that I was raped by someone I loved.

I continued to have hope for the relationship, but the next several months became a series of lies. I was not enough validation for him... he needed that from many other women.

School policies about abstinence in a Christian university, and the political standing that my boyfriend and his family had at the university, ultimately discouraged me from getting help. I realized that going to an on-campus counselor was out of the question, as they might not see things the way I did, and I could end up with a fine or expelled for being a potential threat to scandal.

I took a job waiting tables so I could go on a mission trip to Africa. I tried a little harder with music. I kept on. The relationship ended. What I really needed was counseling and help, but I couldn't bring myself to do it.

So, I began to journal. The numbness began to set in as I cried myself to sleep. But then, during this time, something miraculous happened. I began to dream. This time I wasn't daydreaming with my head in the clouds, I was really dreaming—falling asleep and having the most beautiful dreams, dreams about heaven! It was nothing like what I heard or imagined, with robotic saints floating around in white robes... no.

This dream was a journey from across an ocean that lead me to a beautiful meadow of horses that was given to me! Now, even if you think this isn't that exciting, it was for me! I loved the dream and it was recurring.

God was showing his infinite love for me through taking me on this journey in my sleep. And I was learning... I was starting to wonder what Christian communities could be without dogmatic orthodoxy and ideals. There was so much to process, so much to think about, such as the hard pill to swallow that was forgiving the one who hurt me. Ultimately, forgiveness and healing were a process, but its beautiful beginnings happened in my sleep.

Years went on, I moved back to big city life, leaving the college town behind with all the memories, good and bad. Healing continued to unfold through other friendships, in times of prayer and reflection, and in finding a healthy church community of people that were rare and honest in the beauty of this mysterious thing we call faith. I found myself in the normal ups and downs of life, taking on a corporate job to pay the bills but flourishing as a songwriter—performing and making albums—and rediscovering my love for the city that I left behind for school. I also ended up in a magical and healthy relationship. Though that relationship didn't continue, it was instrumental in the healing process.

Fast forward to 2010, when I was engaged to be married, the dream came again. And a new reality set permanently into my mind and heart: No matter what kind of joy I may find on earth, nothing will be able to compare with the joy God has to offer. His gifts are greater than I can imagine—the dream is just a glimpse. As the scriptures reveal, this truth is for all of us.

"No eye has seen, no ear has heard, no mind can conceive what God has in store for those who love Him."

I am convinced that neither death nor life, neither angels nor demons, neither the present nor the future, nor any powers, neither height nor depth, nor anything else in all creation, will be able to separate us from the love of God that is in Christ Jesus our Lord.

And the story continues.

1. As you reflect on Mari's story, what part stands out to you? What makes this particular part of the story stand out?

2. After reading Mari's story, what question would you want to ask her if you met her personally for lunch at a local café? What makes that question important for you?

3. What would you want to share with Mari if you met her for lunch at a local café?

4. What "religious" things were detrimental to Mari? In your own life?

5. What "religious" things were helpful to Mari? In your own life?

SCRIPTURE

3 Some Pharisees came and tried to trap him with this question: "Should a man be allowed to divorce his wife for just any reason?"

4 "Haven't you read the Scriptures?" Jesus replied. "They record that from the beginning 'God made them male and female.'[a]" 5 And he said, "'This explains why a man leaves his father and mother and is joined to his wife, and the two are united into one.'[b] 6 Since they are no longer two but one, let no one split apart what God has joined together."

7 "Then why did Moses say in the law that a man could give his wife a written notice of divorce and send her away?"[c] they asked.

8 Jesus replied, "Moses permitted divorce only as a concession to your hard hearts, but it was not what God had originally intended. 9 And I tell you this, whoever divorces his wife and marries someone else commits adultery—unless his wife has been unfaithful.[d]"

¹⁰ Jesus' disciples then said to him, "If this is the case, it is better not to marry!"

How does this Scripture describe the relationship that God intended between a married couple?

1. How would you describe the experience of being "no longer two but one"?

2. How do people and our society work to split couples apart? Why do you think this happens?

3. How would having a relationship with a Triune God-Father, Son and Holy Spirit—help people have better relationships with one another?

4. After your reflections on the above story and Scripture, what are one or two next steps you would like to take?

Prayer

I praise you God because you are perfect relationship—
Father, Son, and Holy Spirit. Help me to take steps that lead
to reconciliation with those with whom I am in conflict.
Empower me to do things that create safe and holy space for
others. May your Spirit unite our spirits that we may be one
and still be ourselves.

Amen

Chapter 15
There Is Always A Way
By Dennis Woodard

Prayer of Invitation

*Gracious God, thank you for making it possible for
me to be with you today. Thank you for never leaving
me nor forsaking me.
I invite you to speak to me a word that transforms me.
I invite you to touch within me a spot that needs to be
healed.
I invite you to move me to do the things that you want
done in our world.
Use this time to get me ready for whatever is coming
next.
Amen*

I was married for twenty-five years and have three awesome
daughters—Myshelle, Mikayla, and Myranda. I have been divorced
now for about five years and have been renting a room so I can get
back on my feet financially. At first, I pretty much stayed in my
room doing nothing, not wanting to go anywhere. My landlord
pushed me to get out and meet people. She also suggested trying
some online dating sites. I tried a couple websites and really didn't
like what I saw, at least at first. Then I tried "Plenty of Fish."

The first four ladies that I connected with didn't work out at all.
They had many excuses, including an abusive former relationship, a

broken leg, my closeness with my daughters, and being retired military.

After that, I became very selective of who the next lady I would talk to would be. I saw Teri's bio and liked what I saw. But I was still hurting from the first four rejections. She saw that I had looked at her bio and said hi. I responded and started texting with her, then talking to her on the phone. We set up a meet and greet at a coffee shop in Riverside. We started talking and learning about each other.

She pointed out several red flags that she saw. I asked if we could go out, and she said yes, but I was stuck thinking about all the red flags that she had pointed out. I texted her and told her I was breaking it off because of the red flags I needed to work on. I went to work that night and all I could think about was Teri. The next day I called her and told her that I would like to have a second chance. I felt that God had told me to call her and ask her out. We set up a date to go bowling, as she didn't want to go to a movie and make out! The week prior to going out, we continued talking on the phone. I had told her that I was a pretty good bowler but hadn't bowled in several years and would probably be rusty. She told me that it didn't matter and that she was going to smoke me! I picked her up for our date and she was still telling me about how she was going to smoke me... We went inside the bowling alley, and that's when the fun began, because it became obvious that she was a beginner. I won, despite her trying to distract me!

We continued to date. It was about seven months into our relationship when Teri called me out on information I had bragged about regarding my military career. I had claimed to have performed a job when I hadn't even completed training because I was washed out of the school. I also told her that I held a rank I'd never achieved. I thought that our relationship was through because I couldn't just be myself. I talked to my pastor at church to seek advice on my life that was spiraling out of control.

Teri and I agreed to meet with our pastor together as part of our reconciliation process. God has been very influential in our life, and Teri has forgiven me because of her faith in God.

My faith in God has grown stronger, and I know how much God has given to me. We were married on June 16th, 2018, in Maui.

Teri and I, along with other men and women, volunteer our time with a group of young teen moms who are pregnant and in high school. This group is called Growing Pains. It is a Christian-based organization that falls under the Bridges umbrella and helps to mentor its leaders. We go into several high schools in the area to provide a support system for these kids. We provide weekly meetings at Sierra Vista Community Church where we have a prayer, share a meal, and discuss what is going on in our lives. We have speakers come in from time to time to discuss many things, from how they can better reflect God in their life or properly install a car seat and perform basic car maintenance, to understanding the cycle of abuse and finding health care for them and their children. Some of the young ladies that have been involved after they graduate from high school become leaders as well, and tell their stories and give encouragement to the new girls who come in. We encourage the girls to bring their boyfriends on nights that we don't have a speaker. We separate the guys and the ladies—the ladies do some fun girl stuff together, while the guys have fellowship and talk about guy things, including how God can impact their lives. We provide necessities for them. Some of the young ladies and guys have been around for a while, and some have gotten married and are going to church on a regular basis. God has truly blessed these kids with a way to a better life.

Delight yourself in the Lord and he will give you the desires of your heart. Commit your way to the Lord, trust in him, and he will do this. (Psalm 37:4,5)

9. What problems did Dennis face?

10. How did Dennis overcome those problems?

11. What role did God play in helping Dennis?

12. What problems do the parents in Growing Pains face?

13. How do these young parents overcome their problems?

14. What role does God play in helping these young parents?

15. What problems have you faced in life?

16. How are you overcoming your problems?

17. What role has God played in helping you overcome your problems?

SCRIPTURE

While sitting on the edge of a water well, Jesus has a conversation with a Samaritan woman who has come to draw water in the middle of the day:

{13} Jesus replied, "Anyone who drinks this water will soon become thirsty again. {14} But those who drink the water I give will never be thirsty again. It becomes a fresh, bubbling spring within them, giving them eternal life."

{15} "Please, sir," the woman said, "give me this water! Then I'll never be thirsty again, and I won't have to come here to get water."

{16} "Go and get your husband," Jesus told her.

{17} "I don't have a husband," the woman replied.

Jesus said, "You're right! You don't have a husband- {18} for you have had five husbands, and you aren't even married to the man you're living with now. You certainly spoke the truth!"

{19} "Sir," the woman said, "you must be a prophet. {20} So tell me, why is it that you Jews insist that Jerusalem is the only place of worship, while we Samaritans claim it is here at Mount Gerizim,[c] where our ancestors worshiped?"

{21} Jesus replied, "Believe me, dear woman, the time is coming when it will no longer matter whether you worship the Father on this mountain or in Jerusalem.... {23} But the time is coming-indeed it's here now—when true worshipers will worship the Father in spirit and in truth. The Father is looking for those who will worship him that way. {24} For God is Spirit, so those who worship him must worship in spirit and in truth."

[25] The woman said, "I know the Messiah is coming—the one who is called Christ. When he comes, he will explain everything to us."

[26] Then Jesus told her, "I am the Messiah!"[d] ....

The woman left her water jar beside the well and ran back to the village, telling everyone, [29] "Come and see a man who told me everything I ever did! Could he possibly be the Messiah?" [30] So the people came streaming from the village to see him. (John 4)

18. What things in the woman's life were making her feel so ashamed that she was avoiding the other women of the village and coming to get water from the well in the middle of the day?

19. What made this woman so confident that she could run through the village shouting, "Come and see a man who told me everything I ever did!"?

20. Describe a time in your life when you have experienced freedom from shame. If not, what might help you experience freedom from shame?

21. What are two or three next steps that you would like to explore?

Prayer

Dear God, thank you for coming to this earth to be with us. Thank you for showing us who you are and how much you love us. I acknowledge that there are things I do to push you away. I sometimes have a hard time being myself with you. Help me to trust in your love. Free me from shame. And help me to help others trust in your love.

Amen

Chapter 16
Transformation by Grace

By Ruben Barragan

Prayer of Invitation

*Gracious God, thank you for making it possible for
me to be with you today. Thank you for never leaving
me nor forsaking me.
I invite you to speak to me a word that transforms me.
I invite you to touch within me a spot that needs to be
healed.
I invite you to move me to do the things that you want
done in our world.
Use this time to get me ready for whatever is coming
next.
Amen*

I had no idea my life would be so drastically changed and that I would be where I am today…I mean, just being alive! God's word states: "I shall not die but shall live and declare the works and recount the illustrious acts of the LORD" PSALM 118:17

By all rights in this physical realm I should have been put away for life or dead…stealing anything and everything that was not locked down, doing the unimaginable to women, drinking booze as well as any and all drugs that I could get my hands on. I was addicted to heroin and cocaine (speed ball) for four years. I was also abusing LSD, Quaaludes, pot and the list went on.

I did six months in rehabilitation for heroin and cocaine, and for the first time since the sixth grade I was completely clean and sober. I lost everything…my life, my kids. At age twenty-four, I realized I was going nowhere fast. I felt worthless and useless. I built a wall around myself and made sure no one would ever get in, but I had not yet completely crashed and burned. Six years later I would start abusing alcohol and pot once again.

One day when I was 16, my mother told my family she had cancer and had little time to live. In the back yard of our house I recall yelling at God every curse word I knew and spitting, thinking I could spit on him. I could not understand… "Why my mom?" I said to God, "If you take this from my mother, I will pray to you every day of my life." So that is what I did every day as promised, even on the days I would get high and do other things. I had no relationship with God, but here I was, giving the creator of all that is seen and unseen my demands. Three months later my mother would be pronounced cancer free.

That was the first time I remember experiencing an emotion I had never felt before. Love! I experienced the love of a spiritual being. This was the love of God! Unfortunately, it was short lived. I continually sought this emotional experience through needles, alcohol, bars nightclubs, women, and drugs. This emotion was the most peaceful, sensational experience I had ever felt, but it eluded me for years.

Fighting the demons of loneliness and depression, my addictions to pot and alcohol raged on and consumed me. My dependency started to grow more out of control. By the time I turned forty years old, I was consuming thirty beers, a fifth of Patron Tequila, and a bag of pot, daily, after work. Five years later, once again experiencing feelings of hopelessness, at 4 A.M. February 2007, I had no idea my transformation was to begin. Letting my dog out, I turned the television on and began to channel surf. Why I stopped on a Christian station, only God knew his plan. "For I know the thoughts and plans that I have for you says the Lord, thoughts and plans for welfare and peace and not for evil, to give you hope in your final outcome." Jeremiah 29:11. I began listening to a T.V. evangelist and what he was saying seemed to apply to my life. He just made so much sense and I began to tune in on his program daily. After two weeks of listening, his words were, "Today, you will no longer be able to drink alcohol." I remember thinking, OK. So, after work I started to clean up my shop while the fellas began to arrive for our daily session. I kept remembering the T.V. Evangelist's voice "No longer able to drink" so after my first beer and shot of tequila, I felt like I was gagging. As much as I tried, I just could not take another drink. This totally blew my mind. The next day I experienced the same results.

Continuing to listen to the T.V. Evangelist, another two weeks passed and once again it seemed he was looking directly at me. His words were "Today, you will not get high any longer." Hearing his voice in my head all day, do you know I tried to get high smoking pot. Normally one or two hits and I would be on my way to a good high, but this time nothing. I stuffed that pipe to prove that preacher wrong and finished the whole thing. My friends could not believe it. One of them remarked, "Maybe that preacher put a curse on you."

Hard as I tried to get high for the next few days, I could not even catch a small buzz. Not understanding what was going on, I continued to watch that preacher, talking about something called Salvation— how the Lord had a special calling on my life.

On March 7, 2007 at 4 AM, I turned on the T.V. to the program. In the opening I heard the words of the late Martin Luther King " FREED AT LAST, FREED AT LAST, GOOD GOD ALMIGHTY WE ARE FREED AT LAST!" Then the preacher came out saying; " Today something great is going to come upon you! There is no looking back what is about to take place. You were brought up for such a time as this." At 4:30 AM, he said" Salvation is now! Repeat these words." As he led me into prayer to the Lord! The house was dark, the light of the T.V. illuminating the room, TRANSFORMATION BY GRACE had begun. Do you know I began shaking and crying uncontrollably, but I felt it…I felt that emotion that had eluded me for so many years. His "presence" was so overwhelming, I fell to the ground prostrate, crying, shaking, thinking "why me? Why me? All I have done against you."

And I felt in my heart, The Lord Jesus say. "BECAUSE I LOVE YOU!" The transformation of my life was supernatural, I give all glory and honor to my Lord Jesus Christ! Today I am an ordained Evangelist, traveling around and spreading the Good News of salvation. This is a new beginning, a new chapter of my life. "Therefore, if anyone is in Christ, he is a new creation. The old has passed away; behold, the new has come." *2 CORINTHIANS 5:17* I now have a purpose in my life, to help as many as I can come to the Lord. I never thought the chaotic storm in my mind could ever be calmed. Jesus was the only way for me. I was creating my own destruction, I was going nowhere really, really fast. He is a peace in my heart that I cannot explain. But I do understand this, that if you repeat the prayer below, and mean it from your heart; your life will be drastically changed forever!
There is only one way to find out. Let Jesus come into your heart. If He does not work for you.
THE DEVIL WILL BE WAITING TO REFUND YOUR MISERY!

GROUND LEVEL MINISTRIES

A YOUTH MINISTRY PREPARING FUTURE DISCIPLES. This ministry fights the spiritual assault at ground level, working with troubled teens of every sort. We also serve the homeless by way of feeding not only physical food, but much needed spiritual food as well. Established seven years ago, this ministry meets the needs of the less fortunate-passing out toiletries, clothes, blankets and, above all, the Holy Bible, also ministering and praying for those in need. We have also taught the Word of God to wayward teens at the Phoenix House Academy and now are teaching God's inspired Word in the Juvenile Hall. We believe these are the next generation of Disciples. We have also spread the Word of God on the streets of skid row helping to take brothers and sisters off the streets and into rehabilitation centers. Through Jesus Christ we have witnessed countless miracles, with these adults as well as the children. SO MANY SEEDS PLANTED, SO MANY LIVES CHANGED. BY THE GRACE OF GOD!

If you declare with your mouth
"Jesus is LORD"
And believe in your heart God raised
From the dead, you will be saved.
ROMANS 10:9

1. How would you describe the way in which Rueben was freed from addiction?

2. What are the things that have gained a grip of control in your own life?

3. How did you experience freedom from these things that had a grip in your life?

4. From what do you still need to experience freedom?

5. What would be a good "next step" for you to take towards freedom?

Prayer

Heavenly Father
I come to you in prayer, asking for forgiveness of my sins.
I confess with my mouth; and believe with my heart, that
Jesus is Lord. And that he died on a tree at Calvary that I might
Be forgiven and have eternal life in the kingdom of heaven.

I also believe in my heart that God rose Jesus from the dead
So that I may be saved. Holy Ghost lead me down the paths
Of Righteousness.

IN JESUS MIGHTY NAME
AMEN

Chapter 17
What Are Christians Supposed to Be Doing?
By Jim Milley

Bridges are not structures, but people—people who have been changed on the inside through building deep relationships in a second or third culture. These people carry within them a compassionate understanding of another group of people. These Bridge Leaders have the ability to stand with more than one group: more than one language group, more than one religious group, more than one political party, even more than one country, perhaps even more than one world.

When everything is tearing us apart,

Bridges are bringing us together.

When everything is pushing us into lonely isolation,

Bridges are bringing us together.

When we are utterly alone and afraid,

Bridges are bringing us together.

A Bridge can bring together strangers, neighbors, competitors and even enemies.

And Bridges are inspired by these words of the risen Jesus:

> *"I have been given all authority in heaven and on earth. Therefore, go and make disciples of all the peoples, baptizing them in the name of the Father and the Son and the Holy Spirit. Teach these new disciples to obey all the*

commands I have given you. And remember this: I am with you always, even to the end of the age." (Matthew 28:18-20)

Jesus prays to God the Father:

"As you sent me into the world, so I have sent them into the world....I do not ask for these only, but also for those who will believe in me through their word, [21] that they may all be one, just as you, Father, are in me, and I in you, that they also may be in us, so that the world may believe that you have sent me. [22] The glory that you have given me I have given to them...I in them and you in me, that they may become perfectly one, so that the world may know that you sent me and loved them even as you loved me.

Jesus tells his disciples to:

- Make disciples
- Not churches
- Not worship services
- Not youth programs
- Not children's programs
- Not large buildings
- Not large, full-time staffs

All good things but...

Jesus tells his disciples to:

- Make disciples who can and do
    o Listen to God
    o Talk to God
    o Hear God through Scriptures
    o Feel the presence of God in community

- Obey the commands of Jesus

Jesus tells his disciples to:

- Make disciples
  - Who make disciples
    - Who also baptize
    - Who also teach
    - Who also remember
    - Who also make disciples
      - Who make disciples

The disciples whom are told by Jesus,

"Go."

Could this be what Christians are supposed to do?

Have you?

Would you ask for help to do so?

Today?

A Leap of Faith: Bridges' Founding Story

Jim Milley witnessed it firsthand. During a five-year period from 1995 to 2000, Jim saw a church grow from one to two million members nationwide. Jim was serving in university ministry and leadership development in Ethiopia. The church was the Ethiopian Mekane Yesus Church, a thoroughly Ethiopian-nurtured and led church that sprung up from missionary roots during the communist era that ended in 1991.

Jim noticed that it was more often ordinary Ethiopian Christians that were making disciples and starting new churches. These lay people didn't have degrees or salaries, but they read their Bibles and experienced an intimate relationship with God through daily spiritual practices.

One such leader was Girma. With a high school education and an honorable discharge from the army after being wounded in combat, Girma came back to civilian life with the realization that he had to work on the lowest rung of the economy as a private guard. But he found a way to balance his new work as a guard with a new ministry. More than a few of his neighbors in the slum were HIV positive. Girma brought food, medicine, Scripture, and prayer. He journeyed with them, even through death. He provided for a neighbor's orphaned child. Before long, Girma had a flock of his own to pastor, though he did not have a church salary, church building, large meeting space, or pulpit.

A young graduate discovered that his new government-assigned teaching position was in a town with no Christian church. The new teacher, along with her husband, started a group in their home. They found ways to love their neighbors, as well as her students and their families. Soon they had a flock of their own to pastor, though they did not have a church salary, church building, large meeting space, or pulpit.

Back in America

When Jim returned from Ethiopia after the birth of his second child, who was born with special needs, Jim found that the common practices of Ethiopian Christians were sparsely found in the American church. On the whole, pastors provided spiritual services for members, while the members were less comfortable ministering to people outside the church culture.

God began to stir Jim's imagination. The vision grew slowly. His congregation, the La Canada Presbyterian Church, provided the supportive environment where the vision could grow alongside practical support. Bridges was incorporated on March 10, 2010. In April 2012, the congregation laid hands on Jim, and sent him out to launch Bridges as a mission agency for America.

As we live through a critical time in American history when the pace of economic and social change is accelerating, Americans are feeling increasingly lonely, fearful, and divided. While more and more official churches are closing, many people across America are aware of their need and are seeking something more.

Bridges nurtures and equips local people to serve as Bridge Leaders. This is the best strategy to engage people outside of faith in Christ, particularly those who are not likely to attend an existing church.

As we look out across America, new forms of church are emerging. God is doing something new in our time. All of us identifying with Bridges seek to participate in this movement.

Bridges, a Christian 501c nonprofit ministry, is dedicated to providing the very best support to leaders who make disciples of Jesus and catalyze new Christ-following communities. Bridges identifies leaders and prospective leaders, nurturing and equipping them to disciple people in the many subcultures of America. These leaders and their disciples form new Christ-following communities. This is facilitated through providing services to these leaders, such as 501c3 status, annual assessments, one-on-one coaching, training events, support groups, and accounting services.

Over the past six years, many people have come together and sought to articulate Bridges' vision as concisely and clearly as possible, while acknowledging that Bridges continues to innovate in response to new experiences and the impact of experimental ministries.

Bridges has a dream, a vision, a mission, a purpose, and objectives that guide the movement and represent it to an ever-increasing number of people.

- **Dream:**
  - A transformed America through an ever-increasing number of local Christ-following communities working for the common good.
- **Vision:**
  - Bridges develops leaders who:
  - Befriend, serve, and disciple people outside existing church culture and
  - Catalyze newly Christ-following communities that partner with existing churches.
- **Mission:**
  - Provide the very best support to leaders seeking to make disciples, start new ministries, and facilitate newly Christ-following communities.
- **Purpose:**

- o Discover innovative ways to make disciples of Jesus.
- **Objectives:**
  - o Equip 220 Bridge Leaders by the end of 2020.
  - o Facilitate forty-three Christ-following communities by the end of 2020.
  - o Long-Range 1000 Objectives:
  - o Equip 1000 Bridge Leaders
  - o Start 1000 ministries
  - o Facilitate 1000 Christ-following communities
  - o Make 10,000 disciples
- **Your Opportunity:**
  - o **Contact Bridges to:**
    - ▪ Request more information
    - ▪ Ask about becoming a Bridge Leader
    - ▪ Explore how your congregation and Bridges can partner together
    - ▪ Financially support the Bridges movement
    - ▪ Volunteer to help support our Bridge Leaders
    - ▪ Start a discussion on the topic that interests you
    - ▪ Inquire about Bridges consulting and speaking services

Let us know how this book has impacted your life. Share your story at www.bridgesus.org

Contact:

Rev. Dr. Jim Milley
Bridges dba Network of Community Entrepreneurs
466 Foothill Blvd, #320
La Canada-Flintridge, CA 91011
jim@bridgesus.org
818-299-7622 Phone and Zoom Room
www.bridgesus.org

Made in the USA
Lexington, KY
26 November 2019

57686774R10070